Shaker Fancy Goods

SHAKER SURVIVAL
THROUGH SISTERHOOD AND CRAFT

CATHERINE S. GOLDRING

Down East Books

Down East Books

An imprint of Globe Pequot
Trade division of The Rowman & Littlefield Publishing Group, Inc.
4501 Forbes Blvd., Ste. 200
Lanham, MD 20706
www.rowman.com
www.downeastbooks.com

Distributed by NATIONAL BOOK NETWORK

ISBN 978-1-68475-023-8 (hardcover)
ISBN 978-1-68475-024-5 (e-book)

♾™ The paper used in this publication meets the minimum requirements of
American National Standard for Information Sciences—Permanence of Paper for
Printed Library Materials, ANSI/NISO Z39.48-1992.

*This book is dedicated
to those Shaker Sisters
whose resolve,
resourcefulness, and
unwavering faith
have allowed Shakerism
to persist into the
21st century.*

CONTENTS

Sat. Jan. 10, 1920: *"Always do your best, whatever your hand finds to do, do it with your might, never pass slurred work; never have mercy on or excuse yourself; be lenient to all others; but never measure your own work by a lower standard than the highest. Constantly act as if you would like to be acting if it were the last."*
—Jennie Mathers' Diary, Sabbathday Lake, Maine

Fancy Goods Chapters:

PREFACE

Shaker Fancy Goods: How the Shaker Sisters Survived the Industrial Revolution has been many years in the making, and many more in gestation. I grew up near Harvard, Massachusetts, and the Shaker Village there, so the subject has truly been with me since childhood. I have long admired the architecture and atmosphere found in this special corner of the World.

In pursuit of my interest in American antiquities, I ran an antiques store for many years. That venture led to a long and rewarding friendship with another antiques dealer and collector, who happened to specialize in Shaker Sisters' fancy goods, Nancy Joslin—of blessed memory. Nancy was one of the founders of the Boston Area Shaker Study Group (BASSG), a fellowship of some thirty women and men who live in New England and New York and who share an interest in the many aspects of Shakerism. It was Nancy who introduced me to the BASSG and I soon became a member. She and I became great friends and we went to countless Shaker auctions and spent wonderful times antiquing together. In a very special way, this book is a tribute to our friendship.

Shaker Fancy Goods has two major goals. The first is to give voice to the Sisters' often eloquent, if sometimes terse, journal entries during the crucial years devoted to the production and sales of their crafts. These Sisters speak of their work ethics and their values. Their entries, woven through the contemporary narrative, tell a moving and, at times, astonishing story of communal survival. They document their tireless labors, the successes and mishaps they encountered in fancy goods production, and the journeys they sometimes made to promote sales and purchase raw materials. They also detail the rewards, both financial and intrinsic, that followed sales; correspondence with the public; the establishment of a highly regarded presence in the World's marketplace; and the daily pleasure of working together for the common good. Certain voices will be heard more often—in particular those of Sisters Anna Dodgson (New Lebanon, 1818–1897) and Bertha Lindsay (Canterbury, 1893–1990). Other entries appear as anonymous jottings in the Church Family Records and are equally telling and insightful about a way of life. *Shaker Fancy Goods* describes both the *processes* of fancy goods production and the *results* of these processes.

The book's second and equally important purpose is to present the reader with images of the very best examples of fancy goods through photographs, taken expressly for this book of documented artifacts found in museums and private collections. Every effort has been made to prove the authenticity of these artifacts, many of which are not on display for public viewing. Looked at closely, with an informed eye, they tell their own story, the story of the Shaker Sisters' aesthetics, extraordinary handwork, entrepreneurial energy, and faith in the principles of Shakerism. I am extremely grateful for the cooperation and help from all those individuals and institutions that allowed access to their collections and provided detailed information about these objects. This project would not have been possible without their unfailing generosity and kindness.

Finally, I can only hope that my efforts to honor Shaker women here will make their heroic story better known and better appreciated. Completely counter to the custom of the age, they put the fate of their Communities quite literally in their own hands. With diligence, intelligence, the bond of Sisterhood, and a noble work ethic, they produced—and marketed—goods of astonishing quality and variety. And in doing so, they kept Shakerism alive.

Catherine S. Goldring

Tues. July 24, 1894 *Rains all day. So we lose this day at the
Spring. A loss that cannot be made up. But the rain is good for
the potatoes.*[1]

Sat. June 15, 1895 *The Poland Spring House opened today. This is
but the beginning of hurry and worry, but we must go through
with it in order to have the means to live next winter.*[2]

SHAKER FANCY GOODS

B Y THE MID-NINETEENTH CENTURY, the shift from handmade to machine-made
products had transformed the country's economy: Textile mills and factories proliferated
along major riverways throughout New England, steam trains crossed the country, and
steamboats traveled the waters delivering raw materials and finished goods. For the Shakers, too, the Industrial Revolution brought a dramatic shift in their economic outlook
and prospects. When the Believers could no longer compete with the World's factories
and few Brethren remained to tend to the other occupations, the Sisters turned to hand-
icrafts and domestic products to support the Community.[3] They picked up their needles
to produce what they called "fancy goods" to sell to the World. The Victorian term referred to small, adorned household objects made by women for women.[4] The charm,
usefulness, and quality of the Shakers' fancy goods caught the eye and pleased the taste of
the discerning well-heeled summer tourists who flocked to the grand hotels, resorts, and
fairs throughout New England, New York, and beyond. These items, created with the
industry and attention to form and function characteristic of all the Shakers did, included pin cushions, needle books, black-ash woven baskets, poplar-ware boxes, emeries,
dolls, cloaks, pen wipers, eyeglass wipers, fans, sewing carriers, carpets, horsehair brushes,
and racoon-fur and silk gloves.

The fancy goods trade proved the most enduring of Shaker enterprises. "Small, colorful,
easy to carry, and always useful," fancy goods did brisk sales as souvenirs—and often,
when it came to cloaks, boxes, baskets, and carpets as beautiful, durable home décor.[5] No
farm animals or produce needed to be raised for their production and the goods could be

adapted to whatever machines and labor were available to the Sisters at the time.[6] This lent their wares a variety and charm that continues to distinguish them today. In the early 1860s, for example, Shaker Sisters began to make fancy boxes "by pasting richly colored or patterned papers over cardboard or wooden boxes…. Sometimes one or more sides of a small box were made of glass." Some lids were lined in velvet.[7] Equally unusual, innovative, and income-producing was the invention of poplar-ware cloth that the Sisters wove and made into boxes of various sizes, lined in silk or plush velvets, and, in many cases, fashioned into sewing boxes.[8]

Facing the loss of the agrarian livelihood that sustained their movement, the Shaker Sisters took on the handwork involved in making fancy goods with typical fortitude and spirit.[9] They did this even though they were already busy with domestic tasks that ran from "picking huckleberries in nearby swamps, canning raspberries, churning butter, caring for the sick, and cleaning the hired men's houses, which included exterminating bedbugs." As Sister Anna Goepper of the South Family in Watervliet, New York, wrote in her journal, the Shaker Sisters were "working every minute getting ready for the Christmas sale… almost killing themselves." [10]

Luckily, they soon found a sizable market for their handiwork even though it was not easy to keep up with the demand: "I must hasten for I hope to make between six and seven hundred brushes this spring. This summer will come and the sales, as usual, we must work if we expect to live another winter. The same. Year after year," wrote Sister Aurelia Mace of Sabbathday Lake in her diary in 1896.[11]

But it must have been satisfying to know the fancy goods industry secured the Shakers' survival. Work was a way of life for the Shakers, a form of worship carried out in the spirit of self-sufficiency, harmony, and discipline. As June Sprigg writes, "Sharing work was another important part of the Shaker's worship and way of life. As they worked together to build their barns and homes, they built a spirit of communal love and brotherhood at the same time."[12] This celebratory spirit infuses Sister Matthews' loving description of the close companionship fostered among the Sisters during the winter months of intense labor in preparation for the summer sales: "As we gather in the various sewing rooms, all nimble fingers improving the time that winter days afford by making aprons, holders, and toys, or whatever we feel will interest callers at the Gift shop in the summer. We can here sew, chat, and drink tea, and the time flies all too quickly."[13] Such a clear picture surely conveys the meaning of work to the Shakers, for whom no opportunity to improve the character was ever wasted, and no task proved too small to be instructive. As Sister Jennie Mathers privately instructed herself:

Sat. Jan. 10: *Always do your best, whatever your hand finds to do,*
do it with your might, never pass slurred work; never have mercy

on or excuse yourself; be lenient to all others; but never measure
your own work by a lower standard than the highest. Constantly
act as if you would like to be acting if it were the last.[14]

The Sisters worked all winter to produce the next summer's sales merchandise. They fulfilled individual orders, and prepared enough inventory to display and sell in Shaker family stores and at grand hotels, specialty shops, bazaars, and fairs in Maine, Massachusetts, and New Hampshire.[15] Christmas, then as now (at least at Sabbathday Lake, where a small herb business continues) also proved to be a lucrative time for sales.

Meanwhile, a communal spirit of trade characterized the industry, as many Shaker Villages made similar items and bought both raw materials and finished products from one another. According to Sister Bertha Lindsay, "While different societies originated and manufactured some particular item, these were shared with all others as, while we were like one big happy family, each Society was a complete unit within themselves, self-sustaining, supplying the necessities for their own needs. An interchange of goods from one Village to another was possible because of frequent visits of the leaders." [16]

> **Thurs. March 7, 1894** *Delmer is putting bails on oval boxes. They*
> *are to be lined with satin and furnished with cushions, emery,*
> *and wax for sale. We bought the boxes from Wm. Anderson, Mt.*
> *Lebanon.*[17]

> *Aurelia received a box of fancy work from Eldress Lois Wentworth.,*
> *Hancock, $22.20. The articles are very pretty. Pen wipers in the*
> *form of pinks, chickens, pigs, mice. [Pinks are a type of minnow*
> *or young salmon.*[18]*]*

Most Shaker Villages produced fancy goods, and most Village Families displayed and sold them in their stores frequented by Worldly visitors. The showrooms featured beautiful handmade articles. "The Shaker store is small but tastefully arranged," wrote a reporter for the *Brooklyn Daily Eagle* in 1866.[19] Fifty-six years later, a midwestern reporter offered this charming vignette: "Sister Wetherell… came from behind the counter to show the workroom where she cuts the grasses for her baskets."[20]

The entrepreneurial Shakers generated a far wider circle for their fancy goods in the resorts and grand hotels that dotted the New England and New York landscape. Indeed, their marketplace savvy proved their financial salvation. In the latter half of the nineteenth century, the Shakers copied then popular clothing patterns, and produced several now classic designs of their own (such as the Dorothy Cloak). "The Shaker Goods Department was perhaps the most novel of all. It contained quantities of light and useful articles manufactured by the Shakers,"another reporter from the *Daily Eagle* wrote.[21]

Although it was the Sisters who plied their needles and ingenuity to produce fancy goods, Shaker brethren often accompanied the Sisters on sales trips, at first in horse-drawn wagons, and later by automobile and train. They went as far as Bar Harbor, Boothbay Harbor, Squirrel and Heron islands, Cape Elizabeth, Old Orchard Beach, Lewiston, Belgrade, Bay of Naples Inn, and Poland Springs, and New Gloucester Fair among others in Maine, as well as Raymond in New Hampshire, and Swampscott in Massachusetts. Apparently, their fir pillows made a particular splash at Poland Springs. One late-nineteenth-century journal entry recorded the sale of all their "fir pillows at the Springs hotel."[22]

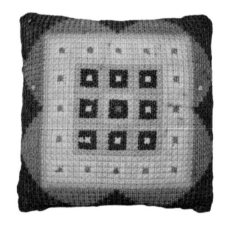

Fir Balsam Pillow
Wool and fir balsam.
6" x 6"; Late 19ᵗʰ C.
Sabbathday Lake Shaker Village, ME.
United Society of Shakers, New Gloucester, ME

In addition to tourist venues, Shakers sold to specialty stores and to private individuals as far away as Canada and New York. In one of numerous letters exchanged between Maine writer Sarah Orne Jewett (1849 – 1909) and Elder Henry Green, of the Shaker Village at Alfred, Maine, Jewett's enthusiasm for the Shaker Sisters' fancy goods is clear. The "work-boxes with handles" she refers to here are wooden carriers outfitted with emery, pin cushion, and needle book.[23]

148 Charles Street
Boston
January 28 [1900]

Dear Elder Henry:

I enclose a cheque for $15, for which will you please ask Eldress Fanny to send this week a selection of pretty things about like those that were sent before. Perhaps there might be a few wooden things added, the work-boxes with handles and a closed box or two. Please direct the package to

Mrs. Henry Parkman
30 Commonwealth Avenue
Boston

and the express shall be paid at this end. I am much interested in a fair here for good objects, and my friends were much pleased with the idea of my getting a box from Alfred.[24] With kind love to all my Shaker friends, I am ever

Yours sincerely,
S.O. Jewett

The Sabbathday Lake Community in Maine made trips to the Poland Springs Hotel several times a week. "The Shakers are familiar personages to the guests at Poland Springs," reports the July 1896 *Hill Top* newsletter put out by the Poland Springs Hotel.

[They make] many visits here during the season, bringing with them a great variety of their goods which their industrious and deft fingers have fashioned during the winter months, when out-of-door occupation is at its minimum. These they display, and the proceeds go into the general coffers of the Community…. Industry is one of their ruling characteristics, and each hour of their waking moments finds some work accomplished or in progress.[25]

In addition, Shakers engaged in a lively business with other mercantile establishments as well as by mail order.

March 5, 1894 *Aurelia sent a box of sale work to Montreal, about $18.00 worth.*

Mon. Sept. 23, 1895 *Large order for Sisters' Work. The Sisters have an order for over $200.00 worth of poplar work boxes also cushions of various kinds. A variety of the little articles that we make for sale. The order is from Annie E. McCarthy, New York City.* **Mon. Nov. 4** *Eldress Lizzie sends a big box of fancy work to the station to go to New York City.*[26]

Jan. 2, 1901 *Sisters finish an order of 130 carriers…and Sisters in office finish off 130 brushes for a southern lady. These articles are all blue and pink.*[27]

Compliments arrived by return mail:

> **Tues. Jan. 6 [1901]** *I received a letter from Mrs. Varney tonight. She liked her new carrier very much.*[28]

In her diary Sister Jennie Mathers recorded a relentless two-week travel itinerary:

> **Mon. Aug. 2** *Sister Prudence and her crew in the work room and I pack and sew. We are all in for a busy week.* **Wed. Aug. 4** *Eldress Lizzie and Sister Prudence and Brother Delmer started for Belgrade lakes this morning to hold a sale.* **Fri. Aug. 6** *Ada and I go to the Springs for today and stay this evening at the Mansion House. We had a fairly good sale not as good as Tuesday.* **Sun. Aug. 8** *Delmer started out for Kineo this morning early.* **Mon. Aug. 9** *Sarah and I start for Rockland and Dark Harbor this morning at about eight o'clock.* **Wed. Aug. 11** *We left Dark Harbor on the early boat and reached Camden at about 10:00. We had a fine sale during the afternoon and evening.* **Thurs. Aug. 12** *We hold our sale here till about ten o'clock and then pack up and go to Samoset…we had a great sale this afternoon and evening.* **Fri. Aug. 13** *We leave Samoset and take the ten o'clock train for home. We come by way of Lewiston and get home about three. Delmer meets us at the station in Lewiston. Ada and Prudence are at the Springs.* **Mon. Aug. 16** *Ada and Iona go on their trip this morning they start at half past nine and go to*

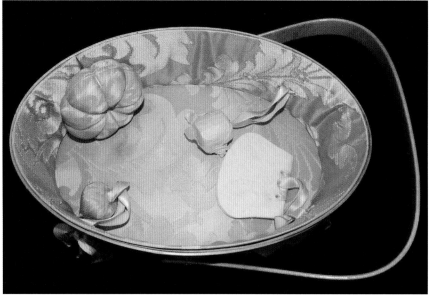

Sewing Carrier (two views)
Wood, copper, silk, wool, wax, and emery.
Made by Brother Delmar.
9" x 6" x 3⅜"; 1953
Sabbathday Lake Shaker Village, ME.
Shaker Museum | Mount Lebanon, NY

Lewiston in the truck and take four trunks with them. Pack the others work in the work room. **Wed. Aug. 18** *Delmer starts on his trip to Scarboro…Prudence and the girls are in all working hard in the work room making more work and lining more carriers.*[29]

On their sales trips, the Sisters would set up decorated tables in hotel lobbies, laying out Shaker items including: woven poplar sewing boxes in a multitude of shapes and sizes; oval carriers fitted with emeries, wax, pin cushions, and needle books; fir balsam pillows; ash-splint baskets; imported dolls dressed in Shaker costumes; horsehair brushes, hooked and woven plush rugs; crochet and knitted fancy goods; pin cushions; and pen wipers. Offering a glimpse of what must have been a Christmas sale at the Thorndike Hotel, in Rockland, Maine, at the turn of the century, a *Boston Daily Globe* reporter wrote:

"Novelties from Shaker Land" was the sign displayed on the window of the Thorndike yesterday which draw crowds of people to the annual sale of the Shaker Sisters, which was opened in the hotel in the morning. The parlors are filled with beautiful articles and garments which a queen might be glad to wear. There is a variety of holiday goods, including Shaker pincushions, Shaker dolls, toilet articles, baskets, and handsome brushes. There are the "Dorothy" cloaks, some of a sober gray while others of the most beautiful shades. There are genuine Shaker sweaters for the men and boys and many orders have been taken for these.[30]

Ten years earlier, another reporter described a similar endearing scene: "Down the side isle are two Shaker Sisters from the Shaker Settlement, Canterbury, 12 miles north of Concord N.H. They are attired in the quaint garb of their quiet sect, and use the quaint old form of speech. They have a collection of pincushions, pen and glass wipers, Angora fur dusters, toys, and candy, all made by the Shaker Sisters.[31]

In the last quarter of the nineteenth century and the first half of the twentieth century, summer sales of the Sister's work made a great contribution to the Sabbathday Lake Shaker Society's income as well as that of other Shaker societies.

Thurs. June 18, 1890 *Pliny getting Fir branches for the office Sisters to make the twigs into the pillows to sell at the Spring house. It is an industry that brings about $100.00 in the course of the summer.*

Wed. July 9, 1890 *Ada and Aurelia go to the Springs. Meet with good success. Sell 9 horse hair brushes.* **Mon. Oct. 7** *Aurelia has taken an order for 500 fir pillows, the .25c size for … They will have them for .20 cts.*[32]

July 25, 1898 *100 spools stands, sold a lot of carriers, dolls, brushes, needlebooks.… Traveled to Cape Elizabeth, Bar Harbor, Bay of Naples Inn, Scarboro Beach Route, Old Orchard, Rangeley route p. 76, Rockland, Bay of Naples, Inn, Portland, p. 109, Squirrel Island Route, p. 76, Kinko route, Poland Springs.*[33]

Success was hard won and the work never-ending, yet it must have been a source of pride and pleasure for the Sisters that the fancy-goods industry sustained their communities at this pivotal time in the nation's economy. This occurred through no sleight of hand, however. As Sister Mathers notes in her diary:

Sat. Jan. 3 *I sew all day and finish the aprons I have been making…I have made twelve aprons.* **Fri. Jan. 9** *I make emeries all the spare time I have today…* **Tues. Jan. 13** *I made 18 emeries since school.* **Sat. Jan. 17** *Make 60 emeries.* **Jan. 20** *Make 80 emeries during the day and evening.* **Jan. 22** *I have made 124 emeries today and finished them. I have made 602 in all.* **Feb. 3** *Prudence and the girls iron poplar today.*[34]

That this cottage industry could compete in the World marketplace seems a remarkable achievement. But then the Shakers, though profoundly spiritual, possessed a canny business sense and the will to turn nature's endowments into a vital source of livelihood. Many years after the fact, Sister Aurelia Mace recalled Mother Sarah Kendall's prophetic words, "The very bushes on Gloucester bear money.… I think of this sometimes when I am selling Fir pillows," continued Sister Mace. "I also think of the time, long years ago when I made the assertion, 'Our money is in the woods.'"[35]

The fancy goods industry offers a singular example of the changing role of women in the post-Civil War era, as they became active participants in the economic survival of their respective Shaker Families. Perhaps most enlightening is the way such vital and necessary work "created a strong bond of Sisterhood among Shaker women."[36] The success of their labors, so crucial to the Society, must have added much to the spirit of camaraderie and ingenuity that bloomed at this time.

WOMEN IN
SHAKER SOCIETY

The United Society of Believers in Christ's Second Appearing began as a breakaway sect in the north of England under the leadership of Ann Lee (1736-1784), an illiterate factory worker turned charismatic preacher who was known to her followers as Mother Ann. In 1774, Mother Ann, moved by a vision (also fleeing repeated imprisonment for blasphemy and dancing on the Sabbath), immigrated to the colonies with eight of her followers. By 1776, at the start of the American Revolution, they permanently established themselves as an independent spiritualist society, in Watervliet, New York, the first village of its kind dedicated to religious worship and organized as a self-sufficient utopian community.

Soon after establishing a headquarters in Watervliet, New York, Mother Ann set out to preach the gospel. More intentional communities modelled on Watervliet were established within New England in New Hampshire, Maine, Massachusetts, and Connecticut. Others followed, as the Believers gained footholds as far west as Ohio, Kentucky, and Indiana.

The Believers came to embrace their popular name, the Shakers, which first arose as a derisive term used to mock their physically active brand of worship, when individuals, inspired by religious feeling and personal revelation, began to shake, tremble, and twist in ecstatic fervor. Outside of these short lived early 19th C. energetic religious observances, they led a peaceful and productive communal existence, living intentionally separate from society, a practice that did not brand them as unusual in their agricultural era.

They practiced celibacy, community of property, and the confession of sin. Being a celibate society and gaining converts meant that their membership grew by two principal means: by the acceptance of adult converts, and by the inclusion of children—adopted as orphans, taken in when homeless, or indentured to the society by parents who could not support them—who grew up in their society and often joined the Shakers when they themselves became adults.

Starting in 1795, after a disagreement about shared property when one of their members elected to leave the Society, all adults who wished to be full members signed the Shaker covenant, which stipulated that all members "have an Equal right and privilege, according to their Calling and needs, in things both Spiritual and temporal." ["Covenant of the Church of Christ in New Lebanon, relating to the possession and use of a Joint Interest 1796," OCIWHi I B 28.] The covenant was originally meant to be a statement of spiritual equality as much as it was a legal disposition of property rights, but it established the tone for communitarian living in Shaker Villages that held all property as a common good.

Confession of sin was a requirement of the Shaker covenant. It was necessary for every Shaker to confess their sins on a regular basis. Elders and Eldressess in their Family would hear confession.

From nearly the beginning, Shaker Communities have been made up of different Families. The Church Family also called the Center Family was regarded as the most avid in the Community. Each Family had its own name such as North Family and South Family and these different families performed different tasks in the village as well as the necessary day to day tasks. Each Family was overseen by two Elders and Eldresses charged with directing spiritual matters within their number. There were also Office Deacons and Office Deaconesses to handle legal matters, later to be called Trustees. Family Deacons and Deaconesses ran the day-to-day operations of the Community enterprises, shops on the premises, orchards, laundry, cooking, etc. Chores were divided evenly between men and women, who performed them separately, not because they believed one sex more physically or intellectually capable than the other in any way, but simply to discourage a closeness that, as one Shaker put it, "would bring men and women into relations we do not think wise." [Charles Nordhoff, The Communistic Societies of the United States (New York, 1875), p. 166.]

The Shakers held themselves to a thorough-going racial and gender equality that was rare both then and now. The original impulse for such equality can be traced all the way to Mother Ann Lee, held by the faithful to be a female counterpart to Christ. This equality was extended in 1796, when John Meacham, her immediate successor, acting on a personal revelation, institutionalized the previously informal pattern for gender equality among the Shakers, a policy remains in place to this day. As he neared death, he rejected the idea of patriarchal succession and named Lucy Wright to take his place as "Elder or first born," their name for the spiritual head of the Community. (Letter from Joseph Meacham to Lucy Wright [1796], OCIWhi IV A 30.)

Eldress Wright proved to be a masterly administrator and advanced and further solidified the principal of equality between the sexes, even as she oversaw the period of greatest expansion of the Shaker Communities. Even after her death in 1821, the equal role of women did not diminish. By that point, the principle of equality was well established. The Shakers chose their leaders according to demonstrated spiritual authority, and that authority was recognized in equal measure in both men and women.

This held true in day-to-day governance as well. Although many final decisions were made by male Elders in ways that reflected widespread practice of the day, Sisters exerted greater rights and powers within the Shaker Villages than women of the World. This was partly due to their greater numbers, a pattern that became undeniable starting in the early eighteen-hundreds, as many men abandoned the communities for opportunities in the industrializing cities of the east or for the promise of gold or land available as the country expanded westward.

The Shakers drew many of their female members from large agricultural families who put a premium on outdoor physical labor and could not always find a place for women as they grew older. Many women from farm families who failed to marry chose to join the Believers, where women were known to play an honored and consequential role. Other women, widowed or fearing the dangers of childbirth or fleeing a marriage that had turned violent, sought refuge in the company of the Shakers, in such number that women of childbearing age typically outnumbered men by anywhere from 2 to 1 to 3 to 1. The overwhelming numerical advantage that women held led the Society to institute a quota system of matching sets of Elders and Eldresess, Deacons and Deaconesses, etc., so that men were at least equally represented in the leadership, if not in the overall head count.

Women also earned another subtler form of equality, owing to their economic contributions. From the mid-nineteenth century on, the main source of income in the Shaker Communities was the production of fancy goods primarily made by the Sisters (although men helped, carding wool, for instance, or cutting black ash or poplar for baskets, especially in the winter, when work of all sorts was by necessity performed indoors). Even before that time the women's contribution to the Shaker Societies was substantial and their voice was heard. Sister Tabitha Babbitt (1779-1853) from the Harvard Shaker Village Community in Massachusetts is believed to have invented what is known as the circular saw, one of the many technical advances now credited to the Shakers.

The fancy good business seems to have grown by degrees. Sister Aurelia Mace (1835-1910) from the Sabbathday Lake Community in Maine wrote about two Shaker nurses who, when required to find a way to pay for a patient's treatment for the settling of a fractured bone, decided to distill and then sell their own mint and rose waters.[37] The Sisters and younger girls were also very involved in the herb and seed business—the Mount Lebanon Shakers were the first to sell surplus seeds, establishing the business in 1794, when it served as the primary source of income for the Shakers before the growth of the fancy goods business. Not only did the women sort, dry, and process seeds and herbs, they also printed their own seed and herb packets, another sales innovation that seems to have originated with them.

When the Shakers invented and then sold nib pens the Sisters added to the incoming revenue by selling pen wipes (which helped a writer avoid splotching clothes or correspondence with excess ink). As these pen wipes grew increasingly more artful, their sales increased. And, as the New England textile business boomed in the beginning of the nineteenth century, the Sisters expanded their offerings of beautifully made sewing accessories such as, emeries, pin cushions, and needle books.

The Shakers differed from other spiritual communities, such as the Quakers and the Amish, with whom they are sometimes confused. The Quakers, who shared a preference for simplicity and personal revelation, did not live in intentional communities like the Amish or the Shakers. The Amish for their part did not believe in gender equality. The Amish also have rejected technological advances, which the pragmatic Shakers have embraced whenever it would lead to greater productivity in line with their insistence on quality and simplicity.

The Shaker Sisters put this principle into practice in many ways. In 1886, the Sisters in the Community in Canterbury, New Hampshire, were approached by an Englishman who asked if they could fulfill a large order of sweaters. The Sisters gladly took on the challenge. After fulfilling that first order for 700 sweaters, the Canterbury Sisters were in the sweater business, regularly updating their capacity by investing in commercial machines capable of keeping up with the increasing demand. (The Sisters finished the collars and seams of the sweaters with artful detail work knitted by hand.)

The Sisters were also the driving force behind a very successful production of the Dorothy cloaks that became sought after by fashionable women of the World, including Mrs. Grover Cleveland, who wore a Shaker cloak, made by the Sisters in Mount Lebanon, New York, to her husband's inauguration in 1893. In 1901, in an attempt to discourage cheap imitations, Eldress Emma Jane Neale (1847-1943) even applied for a patent for the Shaker cloak shortly after taking over the cloak industry at Mount Lebanon, New York.

As they established thriving businesses in a great variety of fancy goods chronicled in detail in the chapters that follow, the Shaker Sisters also ventured out into the World, to sell their wares in hotels and vacation spots and department stores. Without altering their own modest dress or compromising their beliefs, they kept up with changing fashions and pioneered a place for women in the World that was rare for its day and remains an example for industry, ingenuity, and independence.

ACKNOWLEDGMENTS

I THANK MY HUSBAND for his never-ending support through the many years it has taken me to bring this project to fruition.

I am most grateful to Kathryn Liebowitz, for her stellar writing skills and ability to turn my research, writings, and ramblings into coherent essays; to Joe Ofria, for his outstanding photo editing; to Kevin Conley, for his superb copyediting skills, support, and encouragement; and to the incomparable James Brisson, for shaping this collection of text and images into the beautiful design of this publication.

I am grateful to Michael Graham, Director of the Sabbathday Lake Museum and Library, who has provided me with guidance and an essay for this book.

I would like to thank Mr. Nathan Taylor for his collaboration with the basket essay. Mr. Taylor is one of the leading Shaker basket authorities in the country. He has identified all of the baskets in this publication. I am grateful to have worked with him.

There are so many more people who contributed to this effort in essential ways. The kindness shown me by the following individuals in my visits to Shaker sites were as appreciated as they were crucial: Jerry Grant, director of collections and research; Lisa Seymour and Boyd Hutchison, curatorial assistants, The Shaker Museum, Mount Lebanon, New York; Renee Fox, collections manager, Canterbury Shaker Village, New Hampshire; and Lesley Herzberg, curator, and Magda Garbor-Hotchkiss, research assistant, Hancock Shaker Village, Massachusetts; Christian Goodwillie, director of special collections, Burke Library, Hamilton College, New York; and The Shirley Historical Society, Shirley, Massachusetts.

I am grateful for the contributions of the following people as well: Darryl Thompson; Charles "Bud" Thompson; Christine Bertrand; Kent Ruesswick (Canterbury Brushworks); The Western Reserve Historical Society, Cleveland, Ohio; Danielle Peck, senior registrar; Richard Dabrowski, Carolyn Smith, and Michael O'Connor, curator, Enfield Shaker Village, Enfield, New Hampshire; and Chuck Rand, librarian and archivist, and Brother Arnold Hadd, Sabbathday Lake Shaker Community, Maine.

Each of the following added specific information to my overall efforts: Kate MacGregor, publicity director, The Poland Spring Museum, Poland Spring, Maine; Starlyn D'Angelo, executive director, Shaker Heritage Society, Albany, New York; Enfield Historical Society,

Enfield, Connecticut; Alfred Shaker Village, Alfred, Maine; Scott DeWolfe, DeWolfe and Wood Rare Books, Alfred, Maine; The New York State Museum, Albany, New York; Jessika Drmacich, records manager and digital resources archivist, Williams College Libraries, Williamstown, Massachusetts; The Trustees of the Reservations Fruitlands Museums, Harvard, Massachusetts; and The Harvard Historical Society, Harvard, Massachusetts.

Two very kind people have also contributed to my understanding of Shaker communal life: Roben Campbell and Merry Post.

Grateful acknowledgment is made to Karen King for her expertise, passion, and generosity in sharing her contacts with Shaker scholars and collectors. The chapter on cloaks and capes has benefited greatly thanks to Karen's knowledge of the subject and able assistance.

Finally, I want to give special thanks to my entire family for *their* unconditional support throughout.

Catherine S. Goldring

A NOTE ON USAGE

THE FIRST THING THAT READERS MAY NOTICE is the use of capitalizations throughout this book for Brother, Sister, Deacon, Deaconess, Elder, Eldress, Trustee, Community, Society, and Village. Capitalization of the previous words do not apply to quotes in this publication. Thanks to Michael Graham, the director of the Sabbathday Lake Shaker Museum, Michael was able to ask the Believers there about their capitalizations of common nouns. The response he received from Brother Arnold Hadd and Sister June Carpenter was this: "You are representing us—our history—and your work should reflect our customs." This publication respects the Shaker's custom. This publication also uses the word World, instead of world in compliance with the Shaker's use of the word when referring to non-Shaker's; although the shakers have used both.

The text for all the captions follows the following general format: Brief descriptive title; materials; dimensions: length, width, height; date of manufacture, Community of origin and location of object. Community of origin is designated based on existing records and contemporary research.

Shaker Fancy Goods

Above: Post Card Image
North Family Gift Shop
5¼" x 3½"; ca. 1940.
Mount Lebanon Shaker Village, NY
Shaker Museum | Mount Lebanon, NY

Penwipe Dolls
Bisque, wool, silk, and lace, 2½" x 2½";
Early 20th C.
Mount Lebanon Shaker Village, NY
Shaker Museum | Mount Lebanon, NY

1

PENWIPES

Sat. May 19, 1894: *Aurelia [Mace], received a box of fancy work
from Eldress Lois Wentworth, Hancock, $22.20. The articles are
very pretty. Penwipers in the form of pinks, chickens, pigs, mice.*[1]

Brother Isaac Newton Youngs (1793–1865) of New Lebanon made the first
brass-and-silver "one slit" nib pen, with the nib inserted into a holder of wood or tin, in
1819.[2] By the 1820s, pen-making had become a small industry in the Shaker Villages of
New Lebanon and Watervliet, New York.[3] The Shakers used a homemade machine to roll
sheets of metal and scissors specifically designed to cut the slit.[4] Lacking a reservoir for ink,
the quill, and later the metal nib pen, required frequent dipping into an inkwell, and wip-
ing, to prevent the nib from clogging and excess ink from dripping on the page. Penwipes
(called penwipers by the Shakers) made of a sandwich of absorbent cloths stitched together served this purpose.

In the mid 1870s, Shakers, with an eye toward worldly fashion and trends of the period,
adapted the common penwipe as an item for sale around the same time they started making cloaks and capes for the general public; they continued to sell them until the 1950s.
Shaker penwipes took the shape of "pinks" (i.e., salmon), chickens, pigs, mice, pond lilies,
pansies, butterflies, kitties, maple leaves, dolls, bells, mittens, hats, along with simple cut-
outs of chamois cloth.[5] Of the many Victorian patterns for the penwipe then in vogue, the
china bisque doll and pond lily wipes proved the most popular. It is these we find today,
often without any appearance of wear or use, in many Shaker collections. Charles "Bud"
Thompson (b. 1922), founder of the Canterbury Shaker Museum, at the Shaker Village in
East Canterbury, New Hampshire, recalls Eldress Bertha Lindsay making pond lily penwipes until the late 1950s.[6]

These tiny bisque-baked* penwipe dolls, approximately two to three inches tall, had
arms (jointed at the shoulder) with hands, a head, torso, legs, and feet, along with painted
faces, lace collars, and sturdy flared skirts of folded and stitched flannel or wool broadcloth
in alternating dark and light colors. Possessing the charm of the miniature, penwipe dolls

---

* Bisquit (or bisque) baking is a process for firing unglazed pottery that results in a matte finish. This
surface accepts paint more readily.

1

Penwipe Dolls
Bisque, wool, silk, and lace. 2½" x 2½"; Early 20th C.
Mount Lebanon Shaker Village, NY
Shaker Museum | Mount Lebanon, NY

Group of Penwipe dolls
Bisque, wool, and silk.
2¾" x 3"; ca. 1940.
Canterbury Shaker Village, NH
Private Collection

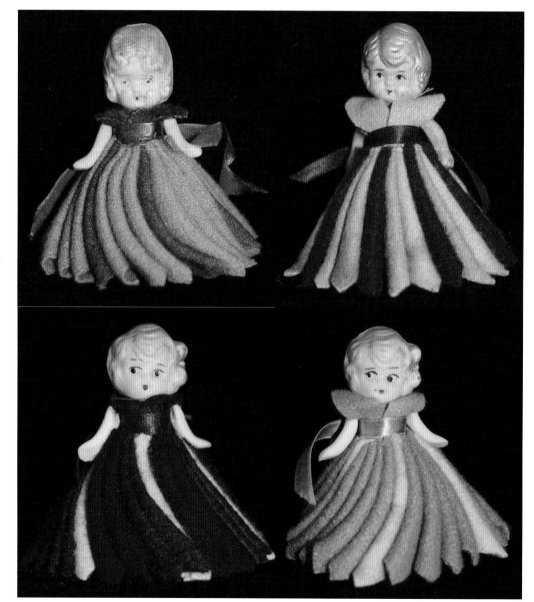

appear to have been a spinoff of the cloak- and cape-making industry, with the skirt material fashioned from leftover scraps of material.[7] The Shakers purchased the bisque dolls from imported sources, unadorned and made in Germany. In her journal, Sister Prudence A. Stickney (1860–1950) notes: "Address for purchases. TINY DOLLS purchased from Boston. . ."[8]

Such dainty penwipes found a place along with pen, ink, and paper on many a lady's writing desk. According to one catalog: "Every lady liked to prepare the pretty trifles which combine beauty and utility."[9] As with all things made by Shaker Sisters, they united form and function, were well-made and eye-catching.

The graceful pond lily penwipe, made from fabric scraps, had a backing of green felt that represented a lily pad. Onto this were stitched two or three rows of white or pink felt petals. A cluster of gold silk floss in the center of the lily represented the flower's stamens. Some Villages varied their color palate for the petals. And, of course, although they used standard patterns, various Sisters added their own individual touches. A pond lily penwipe made entirely of pink cloth, without the green backing is attributed to Sister Ada Cummings (1862–1926) of the Sabbathday Lake Community in Maine.[10] Many Villages made pond lily penwipes, some of which they sold to Sister Villages. In 1890, for example, an accounts book from Mount Lebanon records such a transaction: "2½ doz. pondlilly [sic] penwipers $6.00."[11]

Pond Lily Penwipe. Wool lily pad, 5¼" x 4¼", loop 4"; Early 20th C. Canterbury Shaker Village, NH
Canterbury Shaker Village, NH

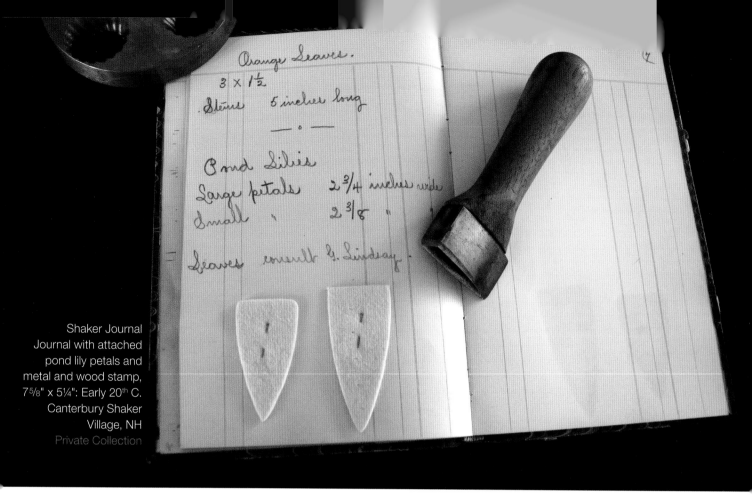

Penwipes were perfect examples of the kinds of modest fancy goods items that attracted the attention of shoppers browsing the sales rooms in Shaker gift shops and other display venues. [12] The first indication of their commercial appeal comes to us from records, kept by the Church Family at Mount Lebanon, of sales work of the Sisters for the year 1876: "Penwipers 72."[13] Their prices were modest: "Mail order of fancy work," a Sabbathday Lake account book reads, "1927 sold 2 pond lily penwipers @ .50."[14] Prices for penwipes varied by only a few cents from one Community to the next. Fancy goods catalogs from Canterbury, New Hampshire, include the following itemized list of penwipes:[15]

Chamois   .20
Hat   .15
Pond lily   .35

And from an earlier catalog from East Canterbury:[16]

Lily   .30
Pansy   .20
Pink   .25

At Sabbathday Lake, by comparison, all the penwipe dolls sold for thirty-five cents. But, small mitten-shaped chamois eyeglass wipers that could double as penwipes, with rhymes printed on them, were ten cents.

Left: Pond Lily Penwipe. Wool lily pad. 5" diam.; Early 20th C.
Possibly Sabbathday Lake Shaker Village, ME
Hancock Shaker Village, MA

Right: Star Penwipe
Chamois, silk ribbon and stitching, 4"; 1889.
Possibly Alfred Shaker Village, ME
Private Collection

Eye Glass Wipe
Chamois sheets, pinked edges, 2½" diam.; Early 20th C.
Mount Lebanon Shaker Village, NY
Shaker Museum | Mount Lebanon, NY

Penwipe
Chamois, silk, and kid leather. 4½" diam.; Early 20th C.
Hancock Shaker Village, MA
Hancock Shaker Village, MA

Interest in penwipes, waned by the mid-twentieth century. The perfection of the fountain pen, with its ink reservoir, controlled ink flow, and screw-on cap (preventing leakage) and the later popularity of the ballpoint pen, initially patented in 1888 by an American, John J. Loud, rendered the penwipe unnecessary. Today it remains a charming relic of a vanished age and a testimony to Shaker thrift, ingenuity, and entrepreneurship.

Pinked Penwipe
Wool, chamois, and silk
2½" x 2¼"; Early 20th C.
Probably Mount Lebanon Shaker Village, NY
Hancock Shaker Village, MA

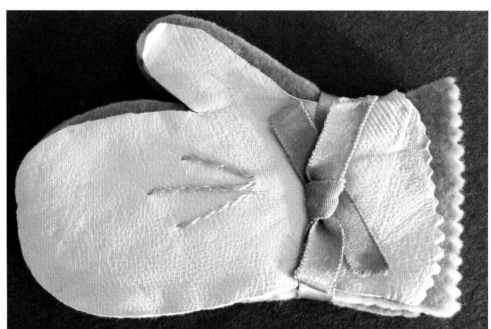

Mitten Penwipe
Wool, silk, and kid leather,
3¼" x 2¼"; Early 20th C.
Hancock Shaker Village, MA
Hancock Shaker Village, MA

Mitten Penwipe or Eyeglass Wipe
Chamois and silk, 4"; Made by Sister Emoretta Belden, Early 20th C.
Hancock Shaker Village, MA
Hancock Shaker Village, MA

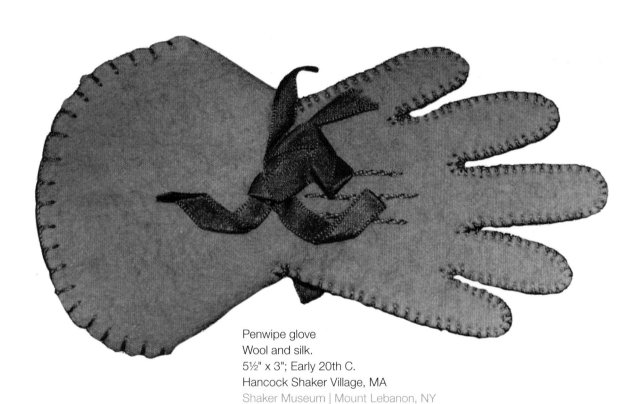

Penwipe glove
Wool and silk.
5½" x 3"; Early 20th C.
Hancock Shaker Village, MA
Shaker Museum | Mount Lebanon, NY

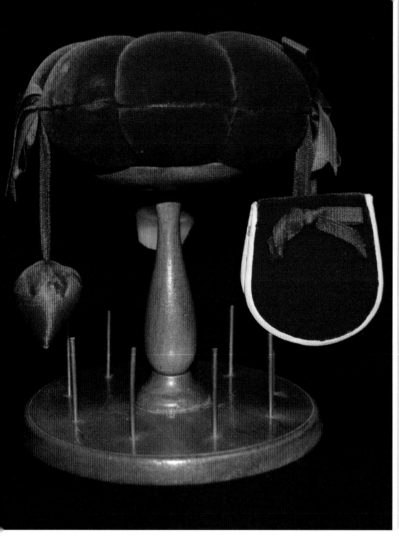

Spool Stand
Pine and cherry wood, iron, velvet, emery, wax and silk.
4¾" x 5½"; 1900.
Probably Sabbathday Lake Shaker Village, ME
Western Reserve Historical Society, OH

Spool Stand
Pine and cherry wood, iron, velvet, emery, wax and silk.
5½" x 5¾"; Early 20th C. Photo by Scott DeWolfe
Probably Sabbathday Lake Shaker Village, ME
or Alfred Shaker Village, ME
DeWolfe and Wood Rare Book Collection

SPOOL STAND, $1.75

Catalog Detail
*Products of Intelligence and Diligence,
Mount Lebanon Col. Co. New York*
7" x 4⅝"; 1908, p.13
Private Collection

Catalog
*Products of Intelligence and Diligence,
Mount Lebanon Col. Co. New York*
7" x 4⅝"; 1908.
Private Collection

PRODUCTS of
INTELLIGENCE
and **DILIGENCE**

SHAKERS Church Family
MOUNT LEBANON Col. Co.
NEW YORK

2
EMERIES, PINCUSHIONS, AND NEEDLE BOOKS

I make emeries all the spare time I have today . . .
— **Jennie Mathers' Diary, 1920, Sabbathday Lake, Maine**

IN THE NINETEENTH CENTURY, sewing at home for fashion and domestic décor became more of a pastime among the newly prosperous and less of a necessity, and when the first dress patterns came into vogue, the demand for needles, pins, and other sewing accoutrements grew at a rapid pace. Indeed, this was the golden age of needle-making in England, a reflection of this demand. By 1824, factories in the Redditch district turned out five million handmade needles each week; by mid-century, they could be made by machine, and that number grew to fifty million a week, making England the number one producer of needles in the world.[1]

The profusion of textiles, some produced abroad, the invention of the sewing machine (in 1846), and the rise of global trading helped make the humble needle into a common household item in America. As early as the 1840s, the Shakers, who were acutely aware of the interest in needlecrafts among fashionable women, began adding decorative emeries–essential for keeping needles sharp and rust-free–to their fancy goods inventory of small sewing items. Emeries were not unique to the Shakers, but the Sisters' versions—attractive, well-made, and fanciful, with a touch of the homespun—turned out to be profitable, along with needle books and pincushions.[2]

In 1879, Brother Otis Sawyer at Sabbathday Lake, Maine, jotted down the prices for Shaker emeries, sold in three sizes:[3]

Emery large .40
Emery medium .25
Emery small .20

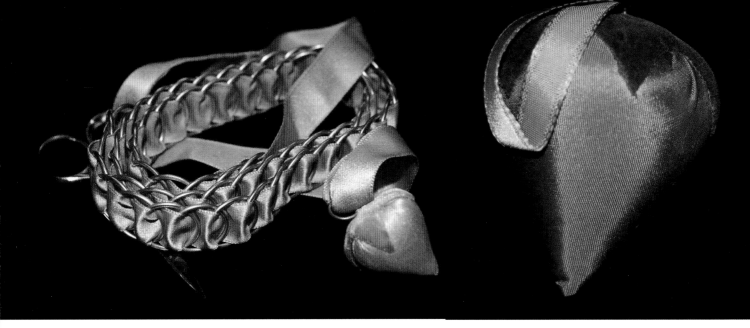

Sewing Chain
Scissors, emery, chain 36" l., and silk ribbon ¾" w.; ca. 1900.
Sabbathday Lake Shaker Village, ME
Western Reserve Historical Society, OH

Emery
Silk and velvet.
2" x 2½"; Mid 20th C.
Canterbury Shaker Village, NH
Canterbury Shaker Village, NH

Emery
Linen, silk floss seeds, cap, and loop.
¾"; Late 19th C.
Probably Hancock Shaker Village, MA
Hancock Shaker Village, MA

The most common type of emery resembled a strawberry, the cover made first of wool, and by the early twentieth century of silk, with either a glossy satin finish or brocaded (satin-woven silk with a raised pattern). The emeries appeared lifelike and charming, with silk floss (later velvet) stem-like caps and embroidered seeds and hulls. In 1910, the Sabbathday Lake catalog of fancy goods referred to these as "Emery balls. Made of satin [*sic*] in different colors with little hulls of velvet, 15c."[4] The process for making emeries resembling strawberry hulls involved cutting and pressing the cloth into wooden molds, then filling each pouch with emery powder—an abrasive compound of corundum (aluminum oxide) used to sharpen needles—before stitching it closed and adding decorative details.

Emeries and Hulls
Wool and velvet.
1" and 1¾"; Early 20th C.
Canterbury Shaker Village, NH
Private Collection

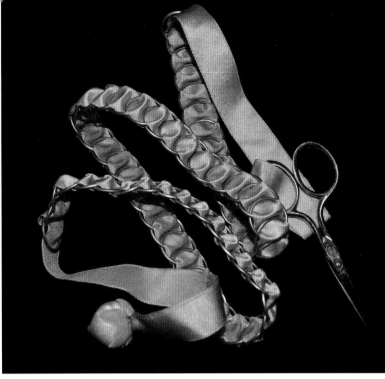

Sewing Chain
Scissors, emery, chain 36" l., and silk ribbon ¾" w.; ca. 1900.
Sabbathday Lake Shaker Village, ME
Western Reserve Historical Society, OH

Many Shaker Communities made daisy emeries, also. The center of the daisy was a round velvet pouch filled with emery powder, the petals were made of felt in complementary colors, and the stem was made from silk ribbon. A 1908 *Ladies Home Journal* article, "What the Shakers Make for Christmas," describes them in this manner: "One of the smallest novelties is the daisy emery. The flower is in yellow and white, with the stem in leaf-green satin ribbon—all pleasingly suggestive of a real flower."

Daisy Emery
(front and back)
White felt petals,
yellow velvet center,
and silk loop.
2¾" diam.; ca. 1910.
Mount Lebanon
Shaker Village, NY
Shaker Heritage
Society, NY

Acorn Emery
Acorn cap and velvet.
1¼"; Early 20th C.
Probably Hancock Shaker Village, MA
Hancock Shaker Village, MA

The Shakers expanded their repertoire to include other naturalistic emeries made to resemble acorns, peapods, and seashells. For acorn emeries, the Sisters used real acorn cups or caps with emery-filled bodies of velvet in earth tones. Apparently, acorn emeries caught the popular fancy. In 1915, the *Detroit Free Press* provided instructions for a do-it-yourself approach:

> Acorn Emery–A little sewing necessity can be made with an acorn cup. A tiny bag shaped like an acorn is made from a small piece of linen or muslin and filled with emery or powdered pumice. Then it is covered again with a bit of brown silk. A drop or two of glue is put into the cup and the brown acorn pressed into place. The acorn emery is then ready for use and is placed among the sewing accessories of the bag or basket.[5]

The number of emeries the Shakers made and sold grew with the years. The Sisters of Canterbury, New Hampshire, produced 107 emery balls in 1847.[6] Records kept by the Church Family at Mount Lebanon show a jump in sales in 1874 when the Sisters sold 800. An erratic pattern of sales there continued:

In 1875, the First Order sold three hundred emeries; in 1876, eight hundred; in 1884, thirty-six; and the following year, eleven-dozen large and small.[7] Meanwhile, emery production at the Harvard Shaker Community continued:

> 1847-07-12 *Thurs. Eliza and Susan draw on a gross of emerys.* [sic]
> 1848-08-10 *Mary began to work on emeries.*
> 1848-08-11 *M.B. & L.B. Work on emeries.*
> 1848-08-12 *M.B. & L.B. finish off 14 doz. Emeries.*
> 1849-08-10 *Simon and Elijah are having Susan put on emery hulls.*
> 1867-07-16 *E. works on emeries finishing them off & carried them to the office.*[8]

In 1873, Sister Anna Dodgson, of Mount Lebanon, noted in her journal: "Emeries 1,000." In the following years she records: "1874 emeries 800; 1875 emeries of all sizes; 1876 emery balls 800; 1877 emery balls 800."[9]

Nearly forty-five years later, Sabbathday Lake Sister Jennie Mathers' diary documents her intense efforts in January and again in December, 1921: "Tues. Jan. 13 I made 18 emeries since school. Jan. 17 [I] Make 60 emeries. Jan. 20 [I] Make 80 emeries during the day and

Emery Hulls
Velvet.
1¾"; Early 20ᵗʰ C.
Canterbury Shaker Village, NH
Private Collection

Emeries
Silk and velvet.
1¼"; Mid 20ᵗʰ C.
Canterbury Shaker Village, NH
Canterbury Shaker Village, NH

evening. Jan. 22 I have made 124 emeries today and finished them. I have made 602 in all. Mon. Dec. 20 I cut out about six hundred emery balls. Mon. Dec. 27 . . . I also began to cut Sister Prudence's [Stickney] emeries and sewed up [name indecipherable] and got her started. Fri. Dec. 31 Stitch up over a thousand emery balls."[10] A year later, on January 1, 1923, Jennie Mathers wrote, "I mend and stitch emeries and make twenty-five this evening."[11]

Shell Pincushions
Scallop shell and velvet
1¼" x 1¼" and 1½" x 1½"; Late 19ᵗʰ C.
Probably Shaker, Community unknown.
Private Collection

Walnut Pincushion
Walnut shell, velvet, and silk.
1¼ x 1¾"; ca. 1880.
Hancock Shaker Village, MA
Shaker Museum I Mount Lebanon. NY

PINCUSHIONS

In the last quarter of the nineteenth century, the Mount Lebanon Shakers Sisters produced pincushions of velvet and merino wool, either tomato- or square-shaped. As with emeries, pincushions were common sewing items and instructions for making them were readily available. An article published in 1954 mentions the Starbright Bluebirds, part of the Campfire Girls, making walnut pincushions for a holiday bazaar.[12]

In England, souvenir trade pincushions included those fashioned from seashells, reflecting the growing attraction and accessibility of seaside resorts. Borrowing from nature, the maker of these sandwiched the pincushion between two halves of a scallop shell, a common practice between 1830 and 1860.[13] During the last quarter of the nineteenth century, records from Mount Lebanon indicate that the Shaker Sisters there produced similar scallop shell pincushions. It seems fair to say the Shakers adopted the design of these appealing items that appear to have originated abroad. American businesses followed suit. In the late 1920s, the Sears, Roebuck & Co. catalog advertised a fancy hanging double [scallop] shell pincushion that sold for twenty-five cents.[14]

According to journal entries at Mount Lebanon:

> 1881 *200 shell cushions by L.Y. [Maker unknown]*
> 1883 *216 shell cushions by L.Y (also emeries)*
> 1888 *75 shell cushions by L.Y., shell cushions by L.Y. 180* [15]

In similar fashion, the Shakers made walnut pincushions using half or whole walnut shells; if the latter, the shells would appear partially opened to reveal the cushion. A coat of clear varnish was applied to the shells to protect them and give them a glossy appearance.

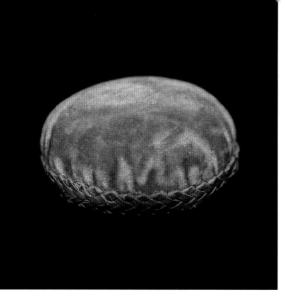

Pincushion
Knitted silk.
2¾" diam. x 1"; ca. 1910.
Made by Sister Emoretta Belden.
Hancock Shaker Village, MA
Hancock Shaker Village, MA

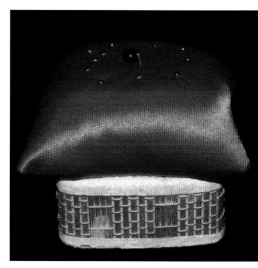

Pincushion
Velvet, wood, and palm leaf braid.
1¾" diam. x 1⅝"; Pre-1860.
Mount Lebanon Shaker Village, NY
Shaker Museum I Mount Lebanon, NY

Basket Cushion
Poplar cloth, silk, and kid leather.
1¾" x 2"; Late 20th C.
Sabbathday Lake Shaker Village, ME
Canterbury Shaker Village, NH

Toilet cushions, as they were called at Sabbathday Lake and Alfred, were velvet cushions with black ash trim. They were used for holding ladies hat pins in an era when ladies customarily wore hats when outside the house. Canterbury called theirs "velvet cushions"; they too had basket trim. Mount Lebanon referred to their cushions as "bureau cushions." Distinguishing features varied from one Shaker Village to the next. The toilet cushions made at Alfred and Sabbathday Lake, for instance, had three brass knobs that served as feet, and they came in three sizes, from 4" to 5½" in diameter.

Velvet Cushions and Box
Velvet, silk, and black ash lace.
4½" diam. x 2½";
Mid 20th C.
Canterbury Shaker Village, NH
Shaker Museum I Mount
Lebanon, NY

Velvet Cushion
Velvet, silk, and black ash lace.
3½" diam. x 2"; Early 20th C.
Canterbury Shaker Village, NH
Private collection

Toilet cushion
Velvet, silk, and black ash lace.
5½" diam; Early 20th C.
Alfred Shaker Village, ME
Private Collection

Canterbury made their cushions in four sizes. Only Mount Lebanon wove a silk ribbon throughout the ash trim of theirs. Canterbury purchased their black ash cushion trim from the nearby Penobscot Indians. The Penobscot called this material lace.[16] Sabbathday Lake, on the other hand purchased their lace or braid, as it has been referred to, from the Passamaquoddy and Penobscot Indians. Mount Lebanon bought their trim from the Mohawk.[17]

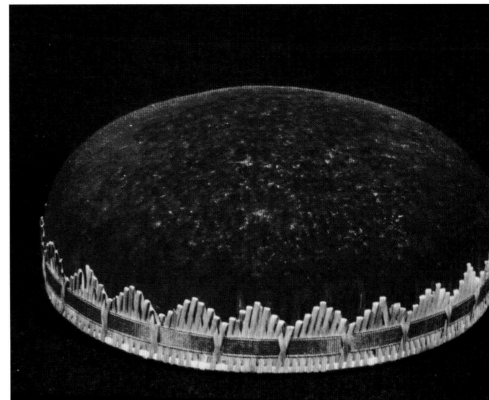

Bureau Cushion
Velvet, silk, and black ash lace.
6⅝"diam. x 2½"; Early 20th C.
Mount Lebanon Church Family,
Mount Lebanon, NY
Private Collection

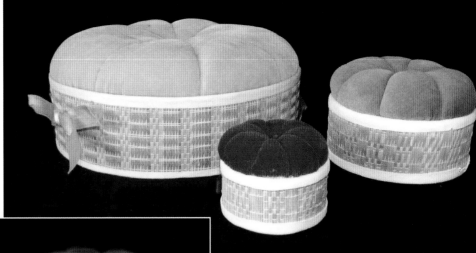

Basket Cushions
Poplar cloth, velvet, silk, and kid leather.
Left to right: 6" x 2½"; 2" x 1¾"; 2¾" x 2";
Late 19th C.
Enfield Shaker Village, NH
Enfield Shaker Museum, NH

Basket Cushions
Poplar cloth, velvet, silk and kid leather.
2⅝" x 2½"; Mid 20th C.
Canterbury Shaker Village, NH
Canterbury Shaker Village, NH

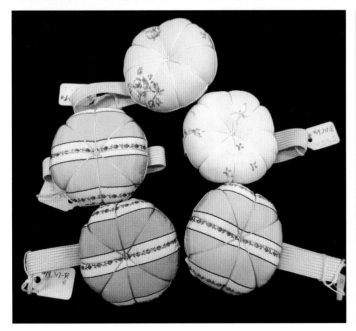

Pincushion Wristlets
Silk and elastic.
2¼" diam.; Mid 20th C.
Canterbury Shaker Village, NH
Shaker Museum | Mount Lebanon, NY

Pincushion
Silk, wax, and emery
2¼" ca. 1940.
Canterbury Shaker Village, NH
Canterbury Shaker Village, NH

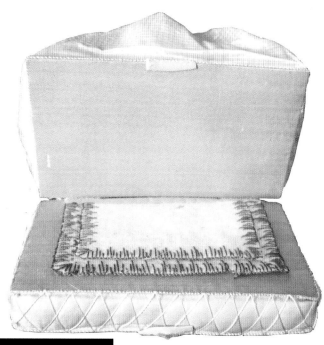

Poplar Pincushion
Poplar wood, velvet, and silk.
"Merry Christmas" in pen and ink
with a drawing of Winterberry
2½" diam. x ⅜"; 1883.
Probably Canterbury Shaker Village, NH
Private Collection

Sewing Bag with Needle Book
Open sewing bag with needle book,
silk and flannel,
3⅜" x 2¼"; ca. late 20ᵗʰ C.
Enfield Shaker Village, NH
Enfield Shaker Museum, NH

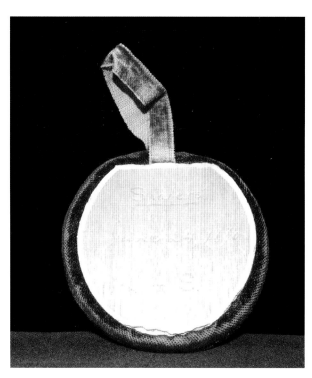

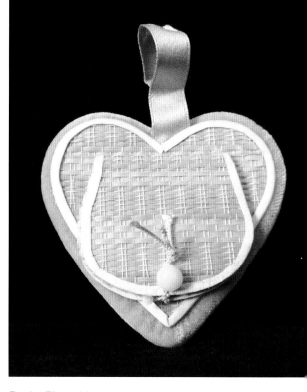

Poplar Pincushion
Poplar wood, velvet, silk, and kid leather. In pencil:
"Shakers/June 24, 1886/L + S"
2¼" x 2¼"; 1886.
Enfield Shaker Village, NH
Enfield Shaker Museum, NH

Poplar Pincushion
Poplar cloth, velvet, silk, and kid leather.
3" x 3"; Late 19th C.
Enfield Shaker Village, NH
Enfield Shaker Museum, NH

Thread Holders with Pincushions
Cotton with cardboard bottom; silk ribbon
strung through spools of thread.
4½" diam. x 2½"; 1930-1940.
Left: Canterbury Shaker Village, NH
Right: Hancock Shaker Village, MA

Pincushion and Needle Book
Cotton, cardboard, and silk.
Pin cushion 1¾" diam.; needle book with felt inserts, 2¾" diam.; 1958.
Sabbathday Lake Shaker Village, ME

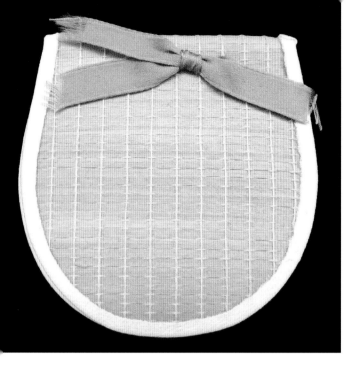

Poplar Needle Book
Poplar cloth, silk, flannel, and kid leather.
3" x 2¾"; Early 20th C.
Mount Lebanon Shaker Village, NY
Hancock Shaker Village, MA

Needle Book
Cotton, cardboard,
felt, and silk.
Made by Sister
Elizabeth Dunn;
2¾" x 3¾"; 1960.
Sabbathday Lake
Shaker Village, ME
Private Collection

NEEDLE BOOKS

To ACCOMPANY pincushions and emeries, the Shakers designed and made needle books. All three sewing items were often made in sets. Needle book covers were made from linen, celluloid, silk, crocheted silk, velvet, poplar-woven cloth, and other materials. Interiors were made from two to six leaves or "pages"—depending on the particular style—of high-quality, thin woolen flannel. The edges of the leaves were either trimmed with decorative stitching or pinked with sheers. Sizes and shapes varied: some resembled figures such as hats, bonnets, bells, hearts, mittens, oak leaves; others were round with a cushion on top. In 1873, Mount Lebanon Sister Anna Dodgson noted the completion of "needle books 600, cushion velvet and merino, tomato and square 1000."[18]

Despite a fire that consumed eight buildings at Mount Lebanon in 1875, needle book (and pincushion) production between 1875 and 1887 continued:

1875 *1st order needle books 200 cushions square and tomato 400*
1876 *Pin cushions 590; Needle books 72; Cushions 20 doz.*
1877 *Pin cushions 20 doz., and needle books 150*
1881 *200 needle books and 106 pin cushions*
1882 *200 tomato cushions, 200 shell cushions, 40 needle books, 23 tomato cushions*
1885 *cushions 200, needle books 110*
1887 *needle books 13 doz., shell cushions 175* [19]

Emeries, pincushions, and needle books, three items found in most women's sewing boxes or baskets, could reflect a sense of order and aesthetic pleasure, in addition to their utility, for their owners. They also expressed a level of quality in design and workmanship we associate now with the Sisters' dedication to perfection in all that they did. The sale of these small items contributed a necessary measure of support to the Shaker economy of their respective Communities.

 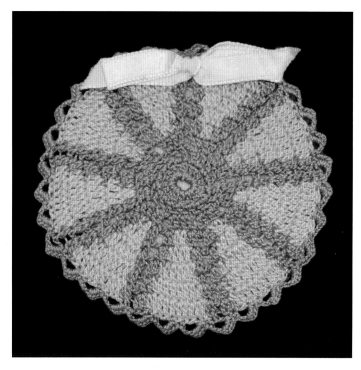

Crochet Needle Book (front and back)
Yellow silk; reverse is blue pinwheel pattern in silk. 3½" diam.; ca. 1910. Mount Lebanon Shaker Village, NY Private Collection

Needle Book
Celluloid, felt and silk; front cover has a painting of Goldenrod flowers. 4" x 3"; ca. 1910.
Canterbury Shaker Village, NH or Enfield Shaker Village, NH Private Collection

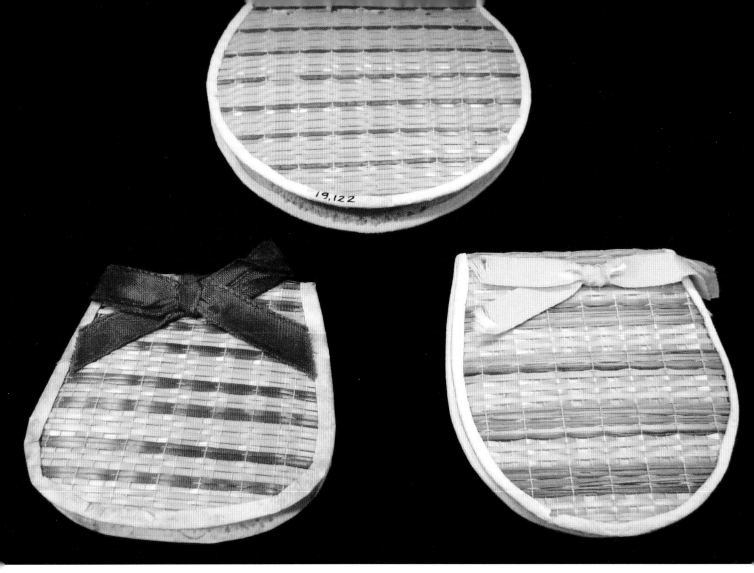

Poplar Needle Books
Poplar cloth, silk, and kid leather.
Top (made by Sister Martha Wetherell), 3¼" x 2¾"; bottom left 2¾" x 1¾"; bottom right 2¼" x 1¾"; ca. 1930.
Mount Lebanon Shaker Village, NY
Shaker Museum | Mount Lebanon, NY

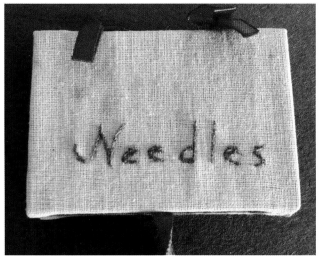

Needle Book
Linen, cardboard, and silk.
2¾" x 2"; Early 20th C.
Hancock Shaker Village, MA
Hancock Shaker Village, MA

Needle Book
Linen, cardboard, and silk. 2½" x 3½" ; ca. 1910. Made by Sister Emoretta Belden, Hancock Shaker Village, MA.
Hancock Shaker Village, MA

Needle Book
Celluloid, silk, and felt.
2½" x 3¾"; Late 19th C.
Enfield Shaker Village, NH
Enfield Shaker Museum, NH

THE FOLLOWING BRIEF PIECE concerning a group of fancy goods "unknowns" to this chapter because the sewing objects described do not fit comfortably anywhere else in the book. It is our hope that some reader(s) will be able to furnish more information about these that can be published in the future.

In 1927, the Canterbury, New Hampshire, Sisters started making and selling intriguing sounding sewing kits that had rather unusual names. Even more fascinating is the fact that we do not know what any of these sewing sets actually looked like, for there are no known surviving examples. From 1927 to 1944, the Canterbury, New Hampshire, Sisters made sewing sets they called Lucettes, Josettes, and Mendettes. Lucettes were cases for spools of thread, Josettes were sewing sets (kits), and Mendettes, darning sets (kits). The sets were made of various richly-colored silks that varied from lighter to darker shades.[20, 21]

No documentation has been found, however, to support the notion that these sewing cases (or sets) were made from pin seal or bronzed leather. Nonetheless, objects made from these materials appear in the antiques market often, are usually called "Shaker," and are sometimes even attributed to the Canterbury Community.

It is possible that these sewing set names originated from the names of two Canterbury Sisters who served as Trustees. A Lucette could have been named for Lucy Ann Shepard and a Josette for Josephine Wilson. The term Mendette could simply be an extension of the word mend.

Sister Josephine Wilson recorded in her diary on March 6, 1928:

Work on sewing sets all day.

Then, five months later:

Tues. Aug. 7 *Work on Mendettes. They are wanted by the 1000.*[22]

Post Card
Interior of Shaker Gift Shop,
Hancock Shaker Village, MA.
3½" x 5½"; ca. 1890.
Private Collection

Pin Safe
Linen, cardboard, and silk.
2½" x ;2¾" ca. 1930.
Canterbury Shaker Village, NH
Private Collection

Crochet Covered Corks
(for knitting needle points)
Silk floss and cork.
Left, yellow 1" h., and right,
pink ⅞" h.; ca. 1900.
Sabbathday Lake
Shaker Village, ME
Western Reserve
Historical Society, OH

Sewing Bag
Glazed chintz cotton, lined with silk or sateen.
9½" diam.; cushion 3½" diam.; Late 19th C.
Enfield Shaker Village, NH
Enfield Shaker Museum, Enfield, NH

Sister Sarle, painting above the
Syrup Shop in northern light.
Photograph on paper.
5½" X 4"; ca. 1950.
Canterbury Shaker Village, NH
Enfield Shaker Villa°ge, NH

3

CORA HELENA SARLE — BOTANICAL ARTIST AND FANCY GOODS PAINTER

*Down the side aisle are two Shaker sisters from the Shaker Settlement,
Canterbury, 12 miles north of Concord N.H. They are attired in the
quaint garb of their quiet sect, and use the quaint old form of speech.
They have a collection of pincushions, pen and glass wipers, Angora
fur dusters, toys, and candy, all made by the Shaker sisters.*
—***Brooklyn Daily Eagle*, August 22, 1866**

IN 1886, NINETEEN-YEAR-OLD Cora Helena Sarle (1867-1956) began composing, in elegant detail, the botanical drawings for a plant journal that for what would eventually be a two-volume catalog, "New Hampshire Gardens," for the Canterbury Shaker Village. The text was written by "beloved spiritual patriarch," Elder Henry Clay Blinn (1824-1905).[1] Indeed, it was Blinn who urged Helena (as she preferred to be called) to undertake this project. She was, he intuited, perfectly suited for the task. She had been living with the Shakers since 1882 and was known to be artistic, sensitive, and in want of an occupation that would improve her fragile health by getting her outdoors.

She began drawing the local plants as a record both of the Canterbury Physicians' Garden, and to teach flower identification to the younger children. By this time, her Community's gardens (laid out by Dr. Thomas Corbett in 1817) were nearly seventy years old and fading, as was their medicinal plant lore and the herbal industry that had served as their inspiration.[2] It was time to capture what remained—for Communal memory and for aesthetic pleasure. Her simple, uncluttered, exact renderings continue to engage and arrest the eye to this day. Coupled with Elder Henry's text, Sister Helena's botanical journals helped to endear her to the Community. Two years later, in 1888, at the age of twenty-one, she signed the Shaker Covenant and committed to the Shaker path that she followed faithfully until her death seventy years later.[3]

More than 180 of her delicate watercolor drawings were gathered in two volumes; these remained at Canterbury Shaker Village throughout her life. Subsequently acquired by a collector, they eventually were returned to the Village, where they are now part of the permanent archives. In 1997, Monacelli Press published a facsimile edition, uniting the original two volumes in one. In her introduction to *A Shaker Sister's Drawings, Wild Plants Illustrated*, Shaker scholar June Sprigg saw a connection between Sarle's botanical representations and Shaker "gift drawings," visual images of spirit messages received by "instruments"—mainly women—during an era of intense revivalism in the mid-1800s.[4] Sprigg, herself an artist, found a likeness in the symmetry, use of space, largely straight stems, and the economical layout of each page.[5] Sarle's brushwork was delicate, her drafting precise, and her ability to express the graceful essence of the living plant—including in some cases its roots—was a calming balm for the spirit.

Sister Helena went on to paint innumerable scenes of Canterbury Shaker Village in all seasons, including the old Meeting House (built in 1792), to sell to the public as part of the Shaker Sisters' fancy goods industry. She painted on a variety of surfaces including tin, glass, cardboard, and fabric. Her delicate watercolors and oils embellished buttons, pin boxes, pin cushions, Christmas ornaments, and tin typewriter-ribbon boxes. She made an abundance of round pincushions with painted scenes on silk with matching velvets. These, as well as her small landscapes depicting rural scenes of Old World charm and sentiment, provided income for her Community. In private work, she decorated electric light globes, umbrella stands, and created larger flower paintings for the Sisters' sitting room in the Dwelling House.[6]

Painting on tin box
Paint and tin.
2¼" x 1⅝" x ¾"; Early-Mid. 20th C.
Canterbury Shaker Village, NH
Private Collection

Painting
Paint and cardboard.
2½" x 2"; Early-Mid. 20th C.
Canterbury Shaker Village, NH
Private Collection

Painting
Paint and cardboard.
2½" x 2"; Early-Mid. 20th C.
Canterbury Shaker Village, NH
Private Collection

Tin (Band-Aid) Box
Paint and tin.
3½" x 3" x 1¼". 1951.
Canterbury Shaker Village, NH
Moriarty Collection

Pincushion
Poplar wood, silk, velvet, paint, and kid leather.
2¼" x ¾" Early 20th C.
Canterbury Shaker Village, NH
Enfield Shaker Museum, NH

Pincushion
Silk, velvet, and paint.
2¼" x ¾"; Mid. 20th C.
Canterbury Shaker Village, NH
Hancock Shaker Village, MA

Pincushion
Silk, velvet, and paint.
2¼" x ¾"; Mid. 20th C.
Canterbury Shaker Village, NH
Private Collection

Pincushion: Canterbury Meeting House
Silk, velvet, and paint.
2¼" x ¾"; Mid. 20th C.
Canterbury Shaker Village, NH
Hancock Shaker Village, MA

Pincushion: Canterbury Meeting House
Silk, velvet, and paint.
2¼" x ¾"; Mid. 20th C.
Canterbury Shaker Village, NH
Private Collection

Pincushion: Lily Pond
Silk, velvet, and paint.
2¼" x ¾"; Mid. 20th C.
Canterbury Shaker Village, NH
Moriarty Collection

Pincushion
Silk, velvet, and paint.
2¼" x ¾"; Mid. 20th C.
Canterbury Shaker Village, NH
Moriarty Collection

Pincushion
Silk, velvet, and paint.
2¼" x ¾"; Mid. 20th C.
Canterbury Shaker Village, NH
Hancock Shaker Village, MA

Buttons
Various sizes and shapes of buttons:
Painted at the age of 87 in 1954.
Canterbury Shaker Village, NH
Enfield Shaker Museum, NH

It is said that Sister Helena's presence remains palpable at Canterbury Shaker Village. Here, visitors can find Sarle's original studio above the Syrup Shop, where the medicines were made and where she worked on the botanical drawings in the 1880s. More of her work may be found in a studio, with her easel still in place, in the Sisters' Shop where she painted in her later years.

In an interview years after Sister Helena's death, Canterbury Eldress Bertha Lindsay (1893 – 1990) recalled with admiration this Sister's dedication to her art and her "beautiful handiwork" on cloaks and other fancy goods:

> Sister Helena Sarle was an artist, and she spent many hours painting in
> a little room at the top of this house, called "The Art Gallery". . . this is
> where she did a lot of her painting as she got the north light which is con-
> sidered the best light for painting. Sister Helena would also do beautiful
> handiwork, like crocheting and knitting, making many articles for our gift
> shop. She also helped out [with] cloak making.[7]

She is remembered by Charles "Bud" Thompson, who, along with three Shaker Sisters, founded the Canterbury Shaker Museum, as a "sweetheart" with a "beautiful, strong [sing-ing] voice."[8] Bud's son, Darryl Thompson, who lived among the Shakers and became an American historian, calls Helena "the village's own Shaker version of Grandma Moses." In fact, he adds, "Many of the Sisters and Shaker-raised children also called her Grammy."[9]

Sister Helena's contribution to the fancy goods industry is unique, a personal expression of a refined sensibility by a tremendously gifted individual, freely offered to the Canter-bury Community in which she played such a beloved part.

Samuel Budd Store
Madison Square, NY; Late 19th C.
Shaker Museum I Mount Lebanon, NY

4

RACCOON FUR
AND SILK GLOVES

. . . down to N.Y. to get the raccoon skins for next season gloves. . .[1]

March 24 *[1883] Wanted 2 pr. Fur stockings, 2 pr. Fur mittens,
1 fur cap to be worn by the captain of the Arctic Greely relief
expedition.*[2]

—Journals of Sister Anna Dodgson, Deaconess Family, Mount Lebanon.

ALTHOUGH THE MOUNT LEBANON, NEW YORK, garden seed industry continued
into the late 1880s or early 1890s, doubts about its profitability cropped up in at least one
Shaker journal as early as 1841. Nonetheless, the industry survived, infused with new energy that lasted from the end of the Civil War until 1870, when the sale of packaged seeds
brought in $7,570.15. In subsequent years, however, this business suffered many reversals.[3]
Well before the 1870s, it faced serious competition from larger commercial growers, at the
same time that the scale of the World's patent medicine industry undercut the sale of the
Shakers' medicinal herbs. By then however, the Mount Lebanon Shaker Sisters had already
added another item to their growing list of fancy goods: coonskin fur and silk gloves for
men.

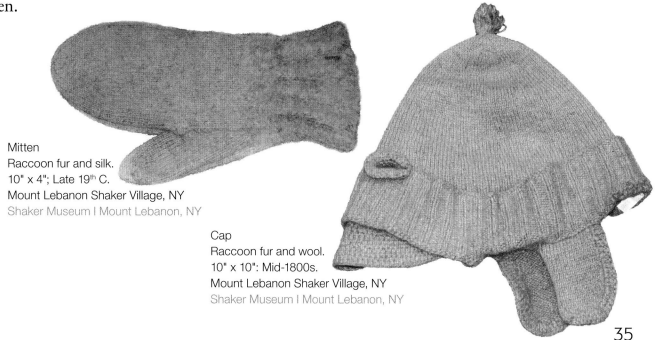

Mitten
Raccoon fur and silk.
10" x 4"; Late 19th C.
Mount Lebanon Shaker Village, NY
Shaker Museum | Mount Lebanon, NY

Cap
Raccoon fur and wool.
10" x 10"; Mid-1800s.
Mount Lebanon Shaker Village, NY
Shaker Museum | Mount Lebanon, NY

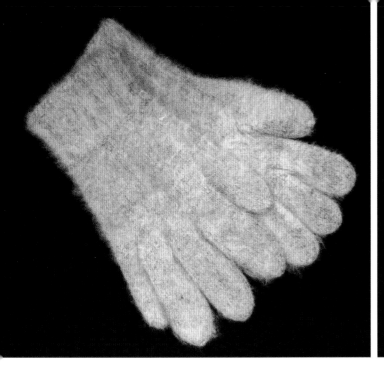

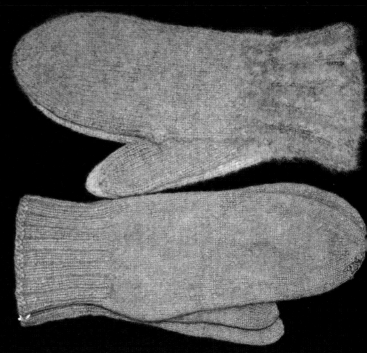

Gloves. Raccoon fur and silk.
9" x 4"; Late 19th C.
Mount Lebanon Shaker Village, NY
Shaker Museum I Mount Lebanon, NY

Mittens. Raccoon fur and silk.
10" x 4" and 9¾" x 3½"; Late 19th C.
Mount Lebanon Shaker Village, NY
Shaker Museum I Mount Lebanon, NY

Mention of the Shakers acquiring coon skins for production first appears in a Mount Lebanon Journal, dated 1869: "coon skins of Jones," followed a year later by, "paid for coon skins."[4]   Yet, it appears from a written record at the Shaker Museum in Mount Lebanon that Sister Mary Hazard knit a "Winter Cap" made of raccoon fur and wool as early as 1850.[5] Clearly, the Shakers had begun exploring the use of these materials to make warm, luxuriously soft items for winter wear well before the gloves proved to be a viable commercial item.

Records from Mount Lebanon (1879) reveal a lively business in fur gloves. "The manufacture of fur and silk gloves has been started on a considerable [sic] large scale by the Ch[urch Family] at Mt. Lebanon and providing the stock for the same is in progress and 100 raccoon skins furred [sic] is now just received to provide fur for the same."[6]

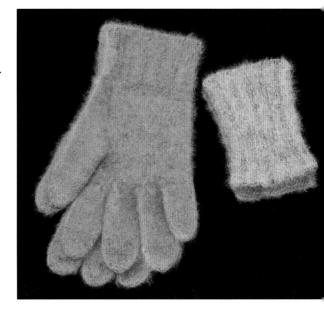

Gloves and Wristlets. Raccoon fur and silk.
Gloves 9" x 4" and Wristlets 4½"; Late 19th C.
Mount Lebanon Shaker Village, NY
Shaker Museum I Mount Lebanon, NY

The success of the coon fur gloves (and to a lesser extent the other fur and silk or occasionally wool items, such as wristlets, caps, "feetings," leggings, and with less success mats, all marketed with a canny understanding of contemporary taste and needs) was synchronous with a feminist shift within the Shaker Society.

The raccoon fur and silk glove production proved to be an exception to the rule of gender separation. Sisters *and* Brethren were involved in this multi-faceted industry, requiring much time, travel, and labor, all meticulously documented in the Shaker records and account books of the period. The Brethren helped with purchasing the coonskins and picking off the fur, while the Sisters took responsibility for delivering the fur and silk to the factory in the town of Hancock, Massachusetts, for carding. The Sisters also did all of the spinning and knitting.

Many hands were needed, and many steps required before the yarn, a fine blend of raccoon fur and silk, could be knit into the gloves that sold for between five and nine dollars a pair. As with all the Shakers did, we know that the labor required to make these warm, elegant gloves was intense, ongoing (in winter and spring), and—of great importance—profitable. The Church Family at Mount Lebanon was the largest contributor to the coon fur and silk industry, with considerable help from the First Order, Second Order, and Office Sisters.

ACQUIRING MATERIALS

JOURNALS FROM THE Church Family at Mount Lebanon reveal the full extent of the work involved, starting with the purchase of coonskins. A page from the Mount Lebanon Community account books from 1888 records the purchase of silk and coon fur [skins] for the making of gloves.[7]

Buying the raccoon pelts or skins involved regular travel to New York City and occasionally as far as Michigan.

1ˢᵗ **order-1877 fur. Nov. 3** *Office Sisters return from New York. They bot* [sic] *fur skins for glove making. Sale work done. FUR GLOVES KNIT 28 pr.*[8]

[1881]
Feb. 22. *100 raccoon skins furred have just received.*[9]

[1883]

Feb. 22 *down to N.Y. to get the raccoon skins for next season gloves.* **March 15** *Mary H and C. Campbell go to N.Y. to meet T.E.Y. for coon skins.* **March 17** *Benjamin, Mary H. and Florinda go to N.Y. to select coon-skins for the fur trade.* **March 22** *Sister with Benjamin return from N.Y.* **March 1** *The sisters return from N.Y.*[10]

[1884]

Feb. 21 *Mary Hazard and Florinda Sears go to New York to buy stock of coon skins for making fur gloves.*[11]

CARDING

A<small>FTER</small> "picking and pulling the skins until the hair was soft and fine enough to be mixed with silk or wool," the rolls of fur, along with purchased silk were taken to a factory in Hancock Village— a small Massachusetts town, completely separate from Hancock Shaker Village—to be carded. This process is still used today for disentangling, cleaning, and mingling fibers and was a necessary step before the Sisters spun them into luxuriously soft yarn.[12, 13]

[1878]

Jan. 24 *the office sisters took a quantity of silk bands, knots, snarls. got from the silk factory very cheaply, and a quantity of fur to the factory in Hancock and had it carded into rolls by machinery, they succeeded well, and a new [season's materials] will be given to the glove business by this move.* **April 17** *Mary Hazzard and Sarah Ann Standish go to Hancock Village to get fur and silk carded and rolled for spinning into glove yarn.*[14]

[1879]

Jan. 28 *the sisters finish getting off fur from 104 coon skins today.* **March 4** *go to Hancock Village north of Lebanon Spring to get the fur and silk carded and rolled by machinery for the glove business.* **April 1** *Office sisters go to factory in Hancock Village to get fur and silk carded and rolled for spinning glove yarn.* **Nov. 20** *Mary Hazard and Sarah Ann go to Hancock to card fur at the mill.*[15]

[1880]

Jan. 17 *Sisters finish fur at tan house, having cut and prepared the fur from 509 pelts.* **Jan. 20** *Office sisters go with Andrew Fortier to Hancock factory to get their fur and silk carded and rolled for spinning glove yarn.* **April 1** *About 30 hands cutting off and picking over fur today at tan house.* **April 2** *the fur hands finish the job today.*[16]

SPINNING AND KNITTING

After the Sisters spun the carded fur and silk into yarn they knit it up into finished, handsome gloves.

—**Edward Deming Andrews**[17]

[1880]

April 8 *go to the factory at Hancock to card and roll the fur and silk for spinning for gloves to be knit. Days spent on fur 40, fur mittens and leggings 4 pr., fur gloves 80 pr. Fur wristlets 16 pair. Mary Hazard spun yarn for 58 pairs of gloves. (Mary Hazard — worked on coon fur 28 days, pick fur and silk and colored silk, gloves 4, leggings 1, mittens 2) Florinda Sears spun yarn for 53 pairs of gloves, knit 12 pr. gloves, picked silk and fur 26 days. One week at tan house, 11 weeks carding fur, two weeks coloring and preparing silk.*[18]

[1884]

March 18 *Mary Hazard and Florinda Sears go to Hinsdale to card and spin the fur for glove making.* **March 22** *Mary Hazard and Florina Sears return from Hinsdale at fur and spinning. Sisters sale work fur and silk gloves knit 267.*[19]

PRODUCTIVITY AND SALES

THE FACT THAT the fur and silk gloves were made for men represents a break in the convention of fancy goods designed primarily for worldly women. For women, these goods fulfilled both domestic needs and their desire for fashionable items of quality, style, and meticulous workmanship. Whether or not the Shakers displayed the gloves with the other fancy goods for sale in the grand hotels and resorts around New England is unknown, but records show the Shakers found an outlet for the gloves in a New York City menswear shop owned by Samuel Budd (1835-1912). Budd was an importer and manufacturer of shirting and an outfitter for gentlemen, with a thriving shop in Madison Square, New York, from 1861. After Samuel Budd died, his son took over the business. Journal entries support the fact that the money for the gloves came from Budd, the sole U.S. agent for retail sales of Mount Lebanon Sisters' work.[20] One from 1888 notes "Budd for fur gloves 469.50."[21]

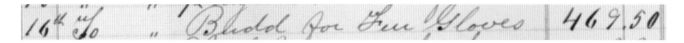

By 1885, Budd's persuasive advertisements for the gloves as fashionable and useful gentlemen's wear appeared in newspapers in Georgia, Louisiana, Illinois, Michigan, and New York State. One ad described them this way: "A specialty is the coon fur gloves for extremely cold weather."[22] According to the Broadcasters Weekly Publishing Company, January 1, 1904, "Samuel Budd's name is an authority upon men's style indispensable to those who wish to be correctly dressed. Nos. 1001–1003 facing on Madison Square, the establishment is seen by every visitor to New York from all points of the compass."[23]

Newspaper Advertisement
Black ink on newsprint.
Atlanta Constitution, Atlanta, GA,
November 29, 1885.
Copyright @ 2016 newspspers.com

Label
Black ink on yellow paper.
4" x 2"; ca. 1890.
Mount Lebanon Shaker Village, NY
Shaker Museum I Mount Lebanon, NY

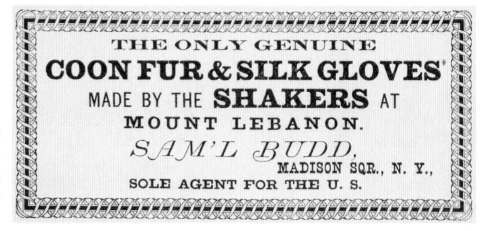

Occasionally, all was not perfect with the coon fur venture. Issues with processing and materials surfaced, or the work proved disruptive, as the following journal entries show:

> [1882]
>
> **Nov. 24** *Mary has re-dyed the fur glove yarn making a great commotion in the fur glove business.* **Dec. 2** *Mary has dyed the yarn which improved the looks of the gloves, but the yarn has to be repacked.* **Dec.** *Our fur was not properly picked so we have consumed a great deal of time preparing the yarn for knitting, days and weeks would not tell the time faithfully improved in picking yarn.*[24]

> [1883]
>
> **April 17** *Mary and Phoebe go to the factory to card the fur. An attempt is made to spin it.* **April 21** *The attempt to spin the fur proves a failure.*[25]

> [1884]
>
> **Sept. 24** *Work on fur continues unabated as yet some at center F[amily] seem rather inclined to move slowly.*[26] **Sept. 29** *The sisters finish the fur picking, a hard, long job, 200 skins picked, or more.*[27]

> [1886]
>
> **Sept. 21** *The yarn not being cleaned is rescoured* [sic] [28]

Such snags in the process appear infrequently. In general, output was prodigious, as these entries show:

> [1879]
>
> **Jan. 28** *The sisters finish getting off fur from 104 coon skins today.* **March 4** *go to Hancock Village north of Lebanon Springs to get the fur and silk carded and rolled by machinery for the glove business.* **April 1** *Office sisters go to factory in Hancock Village to get fur and silk carded and rolled for spinning glove yarn.* **Nov. 20** *Mary Hazard and Sarah Ann go to Hancock to card fur at the mill.*[29]

The records kept by Anna Dodgson (1818–1897), who joined the New Lebanon Church Family's First Order and served as a dyer, weaver, bonnet and basket maker, schoolteacher, and Deaconess, reveal the extent to which the Sisters devoted their time and energy to making the gloves, and the amount of money they earned:

> **[1882]**
>
> **Dec. 1** *Sisters are very much engaged in their fur business to make fur and silk gloves for sale, as they have orders for over 120 pair at $5.00 per pair.* **Dec. 18** *the sisters finish the knitting of 200 pairs of fur gloves, they sell for $5.00 per pair.* [Using the Consumer Price Index, this would equal $ 127.50 in 2018]
>
> **[1883]**
>
> **April 5** *All hands commenced on the fur.* **April 9** *we have been obliged to leave our business at the medicine shop to get the fur along, the second family are putting up the barks, they will continue giving us 4 weeks* [sic] *vacation, at least that is the present calculation.* **April 14** *Shortly after noon we finish the fur. We have worked two weeks about 20 hands. Rachel Simpson 83 years 20 pairs of gloves. Picked the yarn and finished the gloves ready for market.* [30]

During the summer of 1888, the Church Family knit three hundred pairs of gloves. Ten years later, in 1898, the coon fur industry was still going strong. As this entry related to coon fur gloves shows, the work continued to occupy the Shaker Sisters: "It took three weeks for all available help in the Mount Lebanon Center and Church Families to remove the fur from 200 coonskins." [31] A journal entry on May 11, 1903, reads: "Sister Sadie Neale has begun to work up 100 coon skins. Two brothers and two hired women assist in picking skins." [32]

As the nineteenth century gave way to the twentieth, the popularity of certain hand-made items, such as these sturdy gloves, declined due to the proliferation of machine-made goods now readily available in the marketplace. These could be made far cheaper and in many more varieties, thus out-competing all labor-intensive work. But for a crucial period in the Shakers' more than two-hundred-forty-year history in this country, the coon fur glove industry, to which the Mount Lebanon Shakers applied themselves with dedication, added to the other fancy goods the Sisters produced, ensured Mount Lebanon's survival as a viable, relatively self-sufficient Community, dedicated to their chosen way of life.

5
SHAKER DOLLS

Shaker Dressed Doll
Bisque, wool, lace, poplar
cloth, silk, and hair.
Maker Armand Marseille.
12¼"; ca. 1910.
Sabbathday Lake Shaker
Village, ME
Hancock Shaker Village, MA

1901 Sept. 9 *Ada and Lizzie Bailey dress five dolls in Shaker costume. Named for certain sisters the ladies take them readily. They always have the Shaker cap and bonnet and the dress is Shaker throughout.*[1]

—Church Record and Journal, Sabbathday Lake, Maine

IN THE SPRING OF 1949, a *LIFE* magazine story about the Shakers of Canterbury, New Hampshire, sparked a flurry of interest among women all across the country. They wanted to know how they too could acquire a doll dressed like the Shaker Sisters.[2] "Some years ago, I had a doll dressed as you dress, sent to me from Sabbathday Lake, Maine. . . . Now I want more than the doll, I do want a little background. . . . I also would like a doll about nine inches tall wearing your typical silk bonnet," wrote Elizabeth Anthony of Newport, Rhode Island. "Would it be at all possible to get a doll for my little girl[?] I'd be very grateful to you," asked a doll fancier from Ohio. "[I] have long wanted a doll dressed as a Shaker," a retired schoolteacher and doll collector wrote. "Could you make me one about 8" high and what would be the cost?"[3]

Shaker Dressed Doll,
(front and back)
Bisque, kid leather,
wool, silk, and hair.
Maker Armond Marseille.
15½"; ca. 1910.
Sabbathday Lake
Shaker Village, ME
Hancock Shaker Village, MA

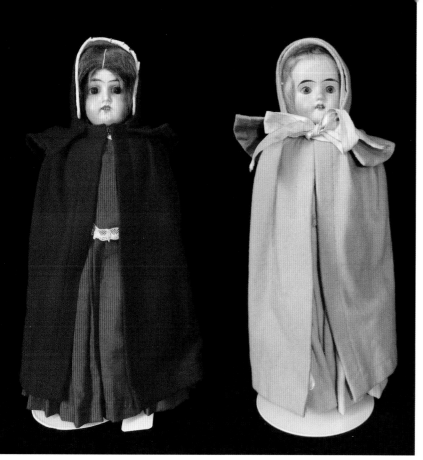

Shaker Dressed Doll
Bisque, woven straw, wool,
and hair. 12"; ca. 1910.
Enfield Shaker Village, NH
Enfield Shaker Museum, NH

Shaker Dressed Doll
Bisque, wool, silk, woven
straw, and hair. 12"; ca.1910.
Enfield Shaker Village, NH
Enfield Shaker Museum, NH

Shaker Dressed Doll
China doll with china head,
hands, and feet.
15½"; Early 20th C.
Mount Lebanon Shaker Village, NY
Shaker Museum I Mount Lebanon, NY

What is astonishing about these missives is not the show of appreciation and requests for dolls, but the fact that the article never mentioned the Shaker doll industry, ongoing since the late nineteenth century. The Shaker Sisters' dolls began as an offshoot of the cloak-making industry, as a way to find a profitable use for their leftover cloth scraps.[4]

Nearly all the New England Shaker Communities created these perfect miniature replicas of the Shaker Sisters, whose clothes included underwear, dress, cap, bonnet, cloak, and shoes, accurate down to the last impeccable detail. The original bisque porcelain dolls made in Germany by Kestner, Simon & Halbig, and Armond Marseille, had glass sleep eyes, wigs of human hair, and hand-painted, lifelike features. (Bisque is unglazed white porcelain with a matte finish that resembles the texture of skin. These dolls were generally fired once, painted, and fired again.) Their hands and feet were bisque as well, with their limbs (often double-jointed at the ankles, knees, wrists, and elbows) and bodies made from kid leather or cloth and stuffed with sawdust. Their porcelain features were beautiful and refined, arranged, as a reporter observed after visiting an exhibition of Shaker dolls in 1911, in a demure expression.[5]

The Sisters also purchased china dolls whose painted black hair and white faces have a glossy finish. China and bisque porcelain, however, were fragile and expensive. Composition dolls, manufactured since the mid-nineteenth century, but more commonly available by the 1920s, represented an advance in the doll-making industry. Composite, which was made from a mixture of sawdust, glue, and materials such as cornstarch, resin, and wood flour, proved easier to work with, more durable, and less expensive than either bisque or china. Early composition dolls had cloth torsos. Eventually, the arms, legs, and torsos that were made entirely of composite.

Shaker Dressed Doll
Composite, wool, silk, and hair. 13"; 1930–1945.
Dressed by Sister Mary Dahm,
Hancock Shaker Village, MA.
Shaker Museum I Mount Lebanon, NY

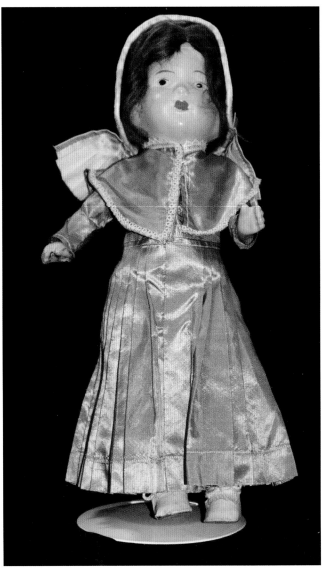

Shaker Dressed Doll
Composite, poplar cloth, wool, silk, and hair. 13"; 1930–1940.
Dressed by Sister Jennie Wells,
Mount Lebanon Shaker Village, NY.
Shaker Museum I Mount Lebanon, NY

Shaker Dressed Doll (front and back). Composite, silk, and hair. 16"; Early 20th C. Community unknown.
Shaker Museum I Mount Lebanon, NY

Doll-making companies, both in America and abroad, embraced composition dolls, which they marketed as unbreakable. Even so, when molded plastic dolls came on the market in the 1940s, they stole the show for being truly robust, softer, and more realistic. The Shakers continued to buy and dress these dolls—though less refined and elegant than their forebears—until sometime shortly after the mid-twentieth century.

Shaker Dressed Doll
Plastic, wool, poplar cloth, and hair.
17"; Mid 20ᵗʰ C.
Probably Hancock Shaker Village, MA.
Hancock Shaker Village, MA

Shaker Dressed Doll
Plastic, wool, silk, poplar cloth,
and hair.
12"; Mid 20ᵗʰ C.
Canterbury Shaker Village, NH.
Shaker Museum | Mount
Lebanon, NY

In 1898, prices for these dolls ranged from between $2.50 to $3.00 each, as seen in this record of the year's sales from Sabbathday Lake:[6]

July 8 doll 1 @ $2.50
July 9 dolls 2 @ $5.50
                     1 @ $3.00
July   1 @ $3.00
                     3 @ $8.00
                     3 @ $7.50

In a more detailed record, Sabbathday Lake Elder Otis Sawyer (1815-1884) left this accounting of earnings from the sale of dolls and their accoutrements:[7]

1898
July

11 cloth for dolls	.39
15 3 dolls for	$8.00
20 dolls	$8.00
25 sold a lot of dolls	
25 doll	$2.50
30 doll bonnets	.70
30 doll	$3.50

August
8 cloth for doll dress $4.26
9 doll bonnets $1.00

1899
July
28 2 dolls $5.00
29 doll $2.50

1905
July doll $4.50

August 30 doll $3.50

Sister Jennie Wells
Photograph on paper.
Sister Jennie Wells with
poplar cloth doll's bonnets,
ca. 1945.
Communal Societies Collection,
Hamilton college, NY

From the Sabbathday Lake *Catalog of Fancy Goods*, 1910, we find this description of the classic Shaker Sister doll, which came in two sizes: a fourteen-inch doll, priced at $3.50; and an eighteen-inch doll, selling for $4.50.

Doll Bonnet. Poplar cloth, and silk, 3½"x 3"x 2¾"; Mid 20ᵗʰ C. Community unknown Private Collection

Shaker Doll Bonnet and Doll Cloak
Wool, silk, poplar cloth, and kid leather.
Early 20ᵗʰ C.
Mount Lebanon Shaker Village, NY
Shaker Museum I Mount Lebanon, NY

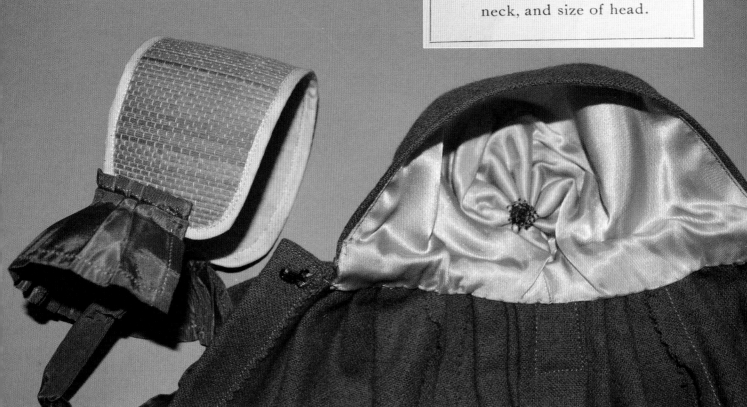

All the dolls are dressed very carefully in the full costume of the Shaker Sister. Their clothes are made of nice cloth and are all removeable. Under the cloak she wears a little silk cape trimmed with a tiny lace. She also wears a pretty little lace cap nicely covered with a woven bonnet.[8]

In the sixteen-page catalog produced by the Mount Lebanon Shaker Community in New York in 1908, *Products of Intelligence and Diligence,* the dolls sold for a bit more "Shaker doll with bonnet and cloak 15" $5.00; and Shaker doll with bonnet and cloak 10" $3.00."[9]

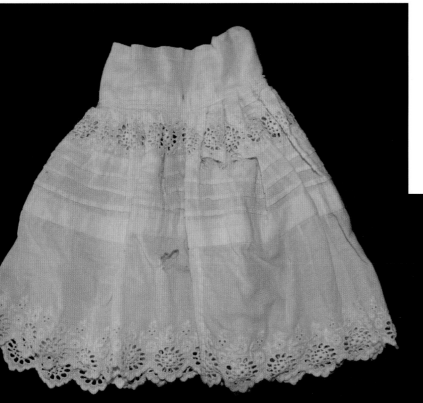

Doll Undergarments
Muslin. 9" x 4"; Early 20th C.
Community unknown
Shaker Heritage Society, NY

In an effort to show the world their fancy goods, sold in the Shakers' Community stores, on sales trips, and by mail order, the Sisters scheduled pre-holiday exhibits at grand hotels around New England. In December, 1911, one such traveling exhibit at the Waldorf Astoria Hotel in Manhattan prompted an article in the *Brooklyn Daily Eagle*. "Yes, gorgeously dressed dolls reflecting the height of Parisian fashion could be found in the usual shops," wrote this smitten reporter, but:

> If you want to find really demure dolls, dolls in long, plain capes, in quaint plaited dresses, in funny little bonnets with frills sticking out at the back of their necks to hide any possible stray curl, you will have to hunt them out in just one place—but they'll be worth while [*sic*] when you get them. . . For these demure young ladies in their grays and their plain dresses are occupying a place that their more elegant sisters well might envy, with no hope of securing except for a chance visit. They are living—for four days— in the Waldorf Astoria, and they are in charge of three women as demure and quaint as themselves and dressed in the same way.[10]

This pre-Christmas exhibit featured dolls from the East Canterbury Community. On display, too, were the Shakers famous Dorothy cloaks in an array of colors. These were very different from the Shaker Sisters' own somber greys, dark blues, and deep crimsons. Also offered for sale were "such trifles as little boxes of sugared nuts and preserved orange and . . . some of the most delightful examples of needlework that anyone would care to see. . ."[11]

As one of the three "quiet, old-worldly sisters," told the *Daily Eagle* reporter when discussing the cloaks: "We have them for children, too, and I must say they look picturesque on the little girls, and there are separate cloaks for the dolls and dresses. We never sell through stores, but we have such a deluge of requests for things by mail that we have all we can do."[12]

Doll prices, along with their separate cloaks, rose slowly with the passage of time. In 1927, the Sisters sold one dozen doll cloaks for $12; in 1930, three such cloaks went for $3.75. That same year, 2 dolls, one pink, and one with gray-blue trim sold for $4.00 each. Eleven years later, in 1941, a "New 12" Shaker doll blue [cost] $5.00."[13]

Two unique dolls that have come down to us as part of the Shaker legacy seem to harken to the American folk-art tradition rather than to the Shaker aesthetic. One, made by a Sister from the Village in Shirley, Massachusetts—deep in apple orchard country—has a head fashioned from an aged, skinned apple, adorned with hair, to which she added a cardboard body dressed in clothing from the World. The other, a double-headed doll listed in the 1908 catalog of fancy goods from Alfred Shaker Village in Maine, includes a White doll which when flipped upside down reveals her Black counterpart!

Although Shaker-dressed dolls appear to be less well-known than many other Shaker inventions and innovations, they clearly charmed the public, in particular women and children. They cherished them perhaps in part for nostalgic reasons and in part for the meticulous quality of the workmanship and for the sheer delight to be found in their winsome charm.

Shaker doll
Apple (head) and silk.
10"; Late 19th C.
Shirley Shaker Village, MA
Hancock Shaker Village, MA

LEFT: Blue Mount Lebanon Cloak
Wool and silk; Early 20th C.
Mount Lebanon Shaker Village, NY

CENTER: Red Dorothy Cloak
Wool and silk; Early 20th C.
Canterbury Shaker Village, NH

RIGHT: Blue Cloak
Wool and silk; Late 19th, early 20th C.
Community unknown

Hancock Shaker Village, MA

6

THE SHAKER CLOAK

1901 April Thurs. 18 *Sisters sell two Shaker cloaks.*
This is the beginning.[1]

— **Sabbathday Lake, Maine**

Sept. 25, 1902 *We that work on the cloaks have to make our*
fingers fly to keep up with the orders. Very little time for reading
and mind culture![2]

— **Mount Lebanon, New York**

DECADES BEFORE THE SHAKER CLOAK became fashionable and sought after by women of the World, the Shaker Sisters wore cloaks to protect against inclement weather. Two cloaks, "grey and drab," top the list of 130 items deemed proper attire for the Sisters (beginning with outerwear and ending with mittens and socks), compiled by a Hancock Shaker Village Eldress in 1838.[3] That same year, a visitor to a Shaker Community commented on the "deep blue riding cloaks" worn by the Sisters.[4] By the 1870s, their cloaks had acquired a distinctive style. Three-quarter length, it was hoodless, made from wool broadcloth (a twill weave pattern), and lined with silk or another wrinkle-proof material. It sported a standup velvet collar, frog (figure-eight shaped) button fastenings, and open armholes with decorative trim. Presumably, it was these cloaks that caught the eye of women of the World who happened to attend Sunday Shaker meeting, did business with the Sisters (on other days), or encountered the garments at the fancy goods displays set up at hotels and resorts throughout New England.[5]

In their heyday, beginning in approximately 1888 (some think earlier), cloaks added much to the Sisters' sales of fancy goods and contributed substantially to the survival of those Villages that were immersed in their production. Although many Shaker Villages engaged in this industry, three stand out in the production of cloaks made for sale to the World: Mount Lebanon, New York; East Canterbury, New Hampshire; and Sabbathday Lake, Maine.

Mount Lebanon made cloaks under the name "E. J. Neale & Co." (for Eldress Emma Jane Neale) with a trademark granted on November 26, 1901. Nonetheless, records indicate that the Sisters there were making and selling cloaks prior to that time under the label

Roll of Cloak Labels. Silk, ¾" h; Early 20th C., Canterbury Shaker Village, NH Canterbury Shaker Village, NH

Clarissa Jacobs & Co., cloak label,
Clarissa Jacobs & Co.
silk, 2¼" x ½"; Late 19th C.
Mount Lebanon Shaker Village, NY
Shaker Museum | Mount Lebanon, NY

E. J. Neale & Co., cloak label,
silk, 2¼" x 1⅛"; Late 19th C.
Mount Lebanon Shaker Village, NY
Shaker Museum | Mount Lebanon, NY

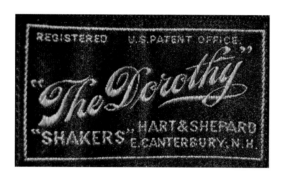

Hart and Shepard, "The Dorothy" cloak label,
silk., 2¼" x 1¼"; Early 20th C.
Canterbury Shaker Village, NH
Hancock Shaker Village, MA

Hart and Shepard, "The Dorothy" child's cloak label,
silk, 2¼" x ¾"; Early 20 C.
Canterbury Shaker Village, NH
Shaker Museum | Mount Lebanon, NY

L.M. Noyes Agent, cloak label,
silk, 3" x 1"; Early 20th C.
Sabbathday Lake, ME
Hancock Shaker Village, MA

"The Genuine Shaker Cloak, *Made by* Clarissa Jacobs and Co., Mount Lebanon, New York." The East Canterbury Community made a cloak under the direction of Sisters Emeline Hart and Hannah Shepard. They called it "The Dorothy" for its originator, Eldress Dorothy Durgin (1825 – 1898) of Canterbury; women of the world sometimes referred to it as an "opera cloak." The Dorothy was granted a trademark in New Hampshire in July 1901. It was in 1901 too that the Sabbathday Lake Shaker Sisters learned the cloak-making business from their East Canterbury Sisters. Sabbathday Lake must have applied for a trademark shortly thereafter; they purportedly trademarked their cloaks under the name "L. M. Noyes" for Eldress Mary Elizabeth "Lizzie" Noyes (1845-1926), a strong leader committed to the manufacture of fancy goods. Noyes, who was an Eldress from 1880 until her death, as well as Trustee and postmistress, joined Elder William Dumont, as the two "led the community through its golden age of prosperity."[6]

MOUNT LEBANON CLOAK MAKING

Making the Shaker Cloak, which is an [sic] unique and comfortable
garment, is one of the principal industries carried on at the present time, and
commands large patronage.[7]

RECORDS SHOW that by 1888 and possibly as early as the 1870s, the cloak industry was well underway. Indeed, Mount Lebanon's sales records from 1888 to 1929 show that Sisters there filled orders for women from as far west as Colorado and Wisconsin, as far south as Arkansas and Tennessee, throughout the Midwest, along the Eastern seaboard, and throughout New England.[8] Cloaks were offered in fashionable colors of the day for the worldly market and proved exceedingly popular through the 1930s. Interest, on the wane since around 1915, declined thereafter to just a handful of inquiries a year.

Though for outerwear, spencers and pelisses—close-fitting, tight-sleeved, waist- and three-quarter-length jackets respectively—often lined or edged in fur, had been in vogue since the turn of the nineteenth century, the Shaker cloak had a certain cachet. It was often preferred by discerning women for fancy dress and eveningwear. Cloaks not only protected the wearer from the elements and the dust and grime of travel, they also kept her then fashionably-wide sleeved dress from crushing. With their graceful, sweeping lines, these garments lent their wearer an air of romance and mystery.

In the late 1880s, under the direction of Sister Clarissa Jacobs (1833–1905), the new industry at Mount Lebanon flourished, keeping the Sisters busy throughout the year. As Eldress Emma Jane Neale (1847–1943), who took over the Mount Lebanon cloak-making industry in 1899, wrote in persuasive letters to her customers:

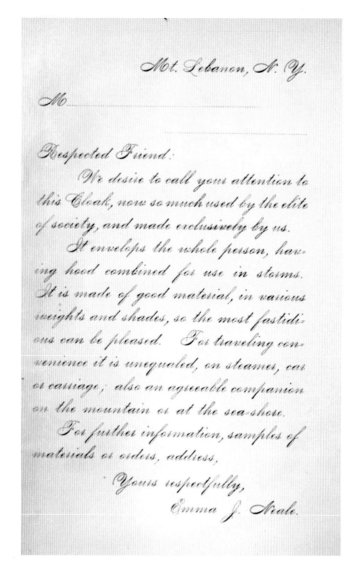

We desire to call your attention to this cloak, now so much used by the elite of society, and made exclusively by us.

It envelops the whole person, having hood combined for use in storms. It is made of good material in various weights and shades, so the most fastidious can be pleased. For traveling convenience, it is unequaled on steamer, car, or carriage, also an agreeable companion on the mountain as at the seashore. . .[9]

As with all their fancy goods, the quality of workmanship, the simplicity of the design, and usefulness of the Shaker cloak proved exceptional. As Eldress Neale notes in her letter (above), its worldly renown had spread quickly to the upper echelons of Society. Indeed, President Grover Cleveland's wife, Frances Cleveland, ordered a cloak from Mount Lebanon to wear to her husband's second inauguration in 1893. The story goes that Sister Clarissa Jacobs made a dove gray cloak for the First Lady, but when the hint of a scorch mark was found in the cloth, another unblemished cloak was hastily stitched to replace it. Much later, the original gray cloak was sold to a collector and friend of the Shakers, so ultimately it did not go to waste.[10]

Shortly after Eldress Neale assumed responsibility for the Mount Lebanon cloak-making industry, she applied for a trademark. Remarkably, just two months after the application was submitted on September 30, 1901, the trademark was registered under the name, "E.J. Neale & Co. Mount Lebanon, N.Y. Shaker Cloak." Such unprecedented speed was likely due to an insider connection: Henry Calver (1845–1943), Brother of Sister Amelia Calver (1844–1929) and himself a former member at Mount Lebanon, served as an attorney in the Washington, D.C., patent office.

Eldress Neale purchased wool for the cloaks from the Russell Woolen Mills in Pittsfield, Massachusetts.[11] In the early years, in addition to the fashionable paler shades, the Shaker cloak came in "Harvard red," "Dartmouth green," navy, gray, black, and white.[12] By the turn of the twentieth century, the range of available colors had broadened considerably to include subtler shades with evocative names such as Albany Cadet-blue, Albany black, fine

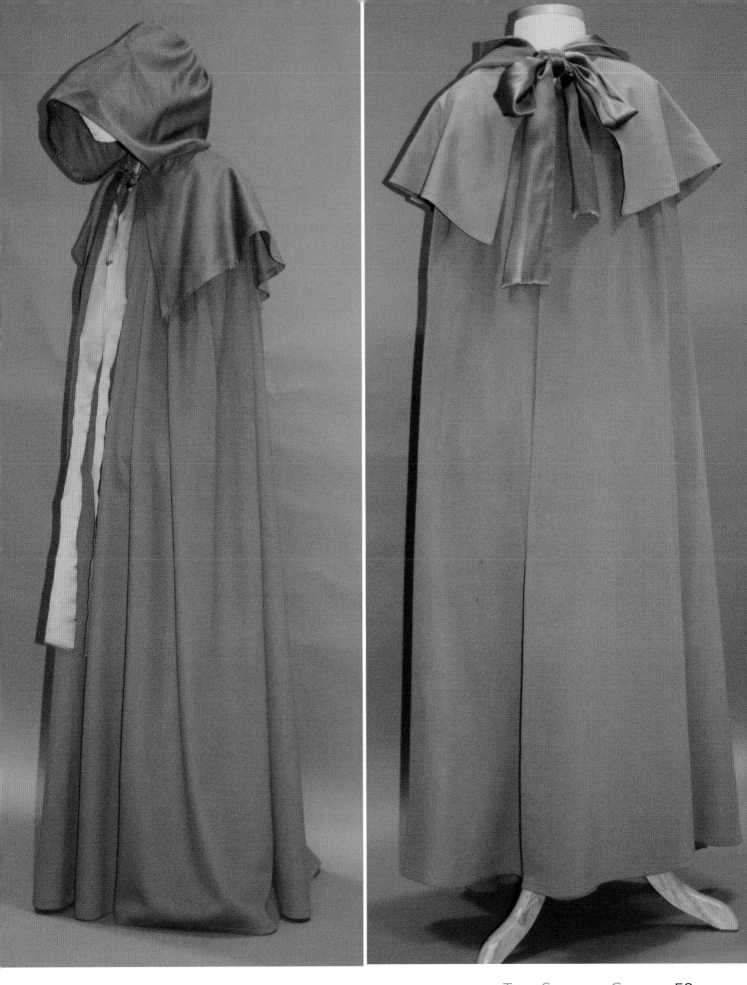

Mrs. Grover Cleveland Cloak (Three views)
Mrs. Grover Cleveland's Cloak
Wool and silk.
49" l.; Late 19th C.
Mount Lebanon Shaker Village, NY
Shaker Museum | Mount Lebanon, NY

Cloak Trademark Document
Black ink and red seal on off-white
paper.
12" x 8"; 1901.
Mount Lebanon Shaker Village, NY
Shaker Museum | Mount Lebanon, NY

Albany black, Russell-tan, new grey, new tan, new red, heavy New York grey, light New York grey, bright New York red, thin New York red, Oxford grey, new seal brown, and more simply, purple, and white.[13] Neale, apparently eager to promote the Sisters' work, secured exhibition space for the Shakers to display their fancy goods in the 1902 Women's Industrial Exposition in Madison Square, New York City.[14]

With such momentum driving this industry at Mount Lebanon, earnings from sales rose dramatically; from $1,556 in 1891 to a record $9,181 in 1899.[15] In the thirty-seven years between 1891 and 1928 the total revenue from cloak sales came to $144,677.

In a record of cloaks manufactured at Mount Lebanon, 1901 and 1902 proved the two most productive years, with the community turning out 295 and 294 respectively. From then on, cloak production gradually declined with only eighty-four cloaks made in 1912, the last year of this particular tally.[16]

While the Sisters made cloaks year-round, September and October proved the busiest sales months. Sister Anna Greaves (1833–1914) of Mount Lebanon left a vivid account of her cloak-making labors in 1902 and 1904, with emphasis on the autumn, when, as she wrote, the Sisters experienced "a rush on cloaks." Of special interest is Greaves' allusion to making a white baby cloak in September 1904.

1902
Tues. Feb. 11 *Work on cloaks, finish off two. This day is mild, no wind. . .*
Sept. 1 *I finish sewing a cloak.* **Sept. 2** *After ironing, finish a cloak, we that are engaged in this business after we get out of work.* **Sept. 23** *I work on cloaks till night.* **Sept. 24** *I finish off a pretty little red cloak. Next sew around a silk white cloak cape in the p.m., finish a black lined*

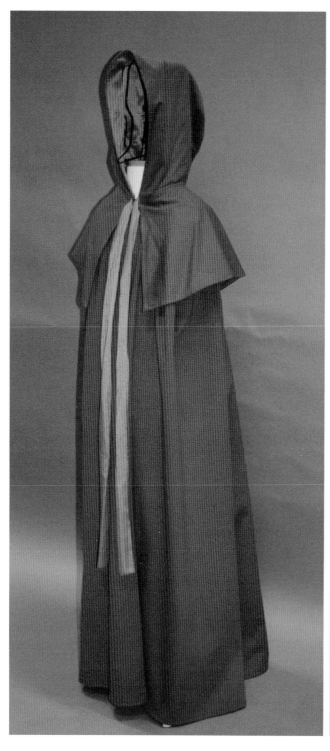

Mount Lebanon Cloak.
Wool and silk.
51" l.; Early 20th C.
Mount Lebanon
Shaker Village, NY
Shaker Museum | Mount
Lebanon, NY

cloak hood, hem a pair of nice silk ribbons. **Sept. 25** *We that work on the cloaks have to make our fingers fly to keep up with the orders. Very little time for reading and mind culture!* **Sept. 29** *Much is done today in pushing the cloak orders ahead. 16 waiting yet on hand.* **Sept. 30** *We are having a rush on cloaks now.* **Oct.** *I am able to sew on cloaks yet, and feel that this helps earn my living.*

1904

Sept.16 *I finish a white silk lined cloak. I was <u>glad</u> when it was done.*
Sept. 19 *Finish a cloak and sew a white baby cloak.* **Sept. 30** *Orders are coming in as many as we can finish and keep up with.* **Oct. 5** *Orders for cloaks are driving us early and late.* **Oct. 14** *I finish a beautiful blue cloak, hood lined with white silk.* **Oct. 27** *This weekend I shall finish off eleven cloaks!*[17]

Postcard
Photograph on card stock.
5½" x 3½"; ca. 1910.
Mount Lebanon Shaker Village, NY
Communal Societies Collection,
Hamilton college, NY

What were the Shaker Sisters earning for their labors? Fortunately, as the years passed, cloak prices kept rising. In 1888, the cost to the public of an unlined cloak came to around $20; in 1896, it ranged around $25; and by 1929, the price had jumped to $40 for a lined cloak.[18]

Cloak sales at Mount Lebanon, 1894. (70Ac3v9 Williams College Special Collections.)

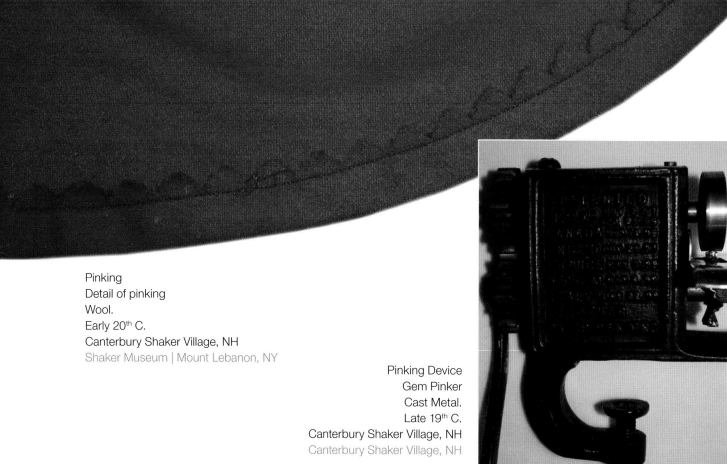

Pinking
Detail of pinking
Wool.
Early 20th C.
Canterbury Shaker Village, NH
Shaker Museum | Mount Lebanon, NY

Pinking Device
Gem Pinker
Cast Metal.
Late 19th C.
Canterbury Shaker Village, NH
Canterbury Shaker Village, NH

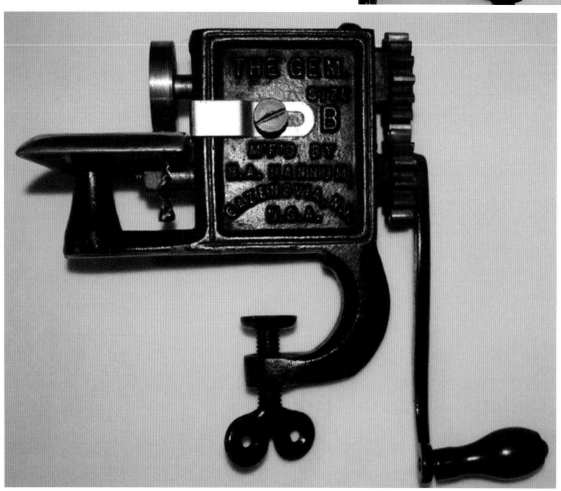

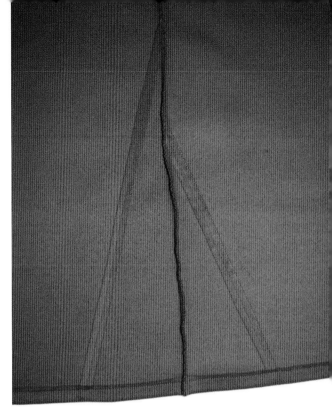

Directions for Girl's Cloaks. French Flannel,

AGE	LENGTH.	NECK	POCKETS	RIBBONS
6mo.& 1 yr.	23 inches.	13.	o	17 in.
2 to 3 yrs.	22 "	13 ½	o	17 in.
4 years.	24 & 25 in.	13 ½	o	19 in.
5 years	26 & 27 in.	13 ½	o	19 in.
6 yrs. gored.	28 & 29 in.	13½	8 in.from neck.	21 in.
7 yrs. "	29 & 31 in.	13 ½	11 in " "	23 in.
8 to 9 yrs.	30 to 33 in	14	11 " " "	24 in.
10 to 11 Yrs.	33 to 36 in.	14	12 " " "	27 in.
12 to 13 yrs.	37 to 38 in.	14.	14 " " "	28 in.
14 years	39 to 40 in	14 ½	14 " " "	29 in.
15 years	40 to 42 in	15	15 " " "	30 in.
16 years	43 to 44 in.	15 ½	16 " " "	30.in.
17 years.	44 & 45 in.	15 ½	16 " " "	32 in.

Children's Cloaks,------- French Flannel.

AGE.	LENGTH.	PRICE.
Infant's, 6mo.& 1yr.(Broadcloth.)	23 inches.	$ 5.00
2 to 3 years -------	22 inches.	---------- $ 5.00
4 years. --------	24 to 25 in.	---------- $ 5.00
5 years. --------	26 to 27 in.	---------- $ 6.00
6 years. gored.--	28 to 29 in.	---------- $ 7.00
7 years. --------	29 to 31 in.	---------- $ 8.00
8 to 9 yrs. --------	30 to 32 in.	---------- $ 9.00
10 to 11 yrs. -------	33 to 36 in.	---------- $ 10.00
12 to 13 yrs. ------	37 to 38 in.	---------- $ 10.00
14 years, -------	39 to 40 in.	---------- $ 12.00
15 years -------	40 to 42 in.	---------- $ 15.00
16 & 17 Yrs. -------	43 & 44 in.	---------- $ 16.00

Silk lining from $ 3.00 to $ 14.00 extra,according to size.

Broadcloth from $ 2.00 to $10.00 extra.

CLOAKS

Dolls'	$0.50 to $1.50
Infants', 6 mo. size, hood lined	2.00 and 3.00
Infants', 1 yr. size, hood lined	3.00 and 4.00
Infants', 6 mo. size, lined throughout	4.00 and 5.00
Infants', 1 yr. size, lined throughout	5.00 and 6.00

Address all orders to

HART & SHEPARD,
East Canterbury, N. H.

All three cloak-making communities were working from a standardized design that included stylish details pleasing to women of the World. Certain distinguishing features help determine a cloak's provenance. For example, Canterbury and Sabbathday Lake pinked the edges of their cloaks using the Hannum Gem 3 pinking machine, a new technology at the time that produced a scalloped edge that was less likely to fray. The Mount Lebanon Sisters cut their seam edges with ordinary scissors for a straight-edged finish.[19] Unique to the industry, their cloaks also had double gussets—triangular-shaped pieces of cloth inserted into each side seam within about six to eight inches of the cloak's hem— allowing necessary additional cloth for a circular hem. These gussets also served to reinforce the cloth. Mount Lebanon cloaks had side-seam pockets, and hood ties of double-sided silk, while the Sabbathday Lake and Canterbury cloaks had patch pockets—slightly wider at the top, and the hood ties had fringed ends (created by unraveling the weft about an inch).

THE "DOROTHY"
OR
SHAKER CLOAK

This unique garment supplies a long-felt want for auto or ocean travel, and in fancy shades for an evening wrap. Made with shoulder-cape and silk-lined hood, the cloak falls in graceful folds to the hem of the dress. A short cape is also made by a similar pattern, prices varying according to length. The cloak may be lined throughout by special order. Samples of cloth and linings furnished on application. Infants' and children's cloaks in the various sizes are carried in stock. (See page 7.)

For further particulars, address

HART & SHEPARD,

East Canterbury, N. H.

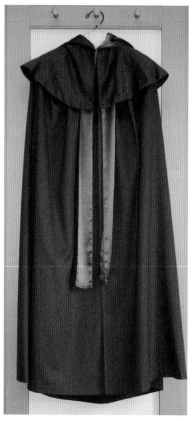

Dorothy Cloak
Circular
Black ink on
off-white paper.
6¼" x 4¼";
Early 20th C.
Canterbury
Shaker Village,
NH
Canterbury
Shaker Village,
NH

Dorothy Cloak (two views)
Wool and silk.
50¾" l.; Early 20th C.
Canterbury Shaker Village, NH
Hancock Shaker Village, MA

THE DOROTHY CLOAK, which gained such a strong following, is attributed to Eldress Dorothy Durgin of Canterbury.[20] Inspired by a raincoat of exemplary design and functionality, Durgin took that garment apart and copied the pattern pieces for what would become the prototype woolen cloak, replacing earlier designs as the standard for Canterbury.[21]

Records show patenting the design to have been a two-step process. In 1901, the trademark on "The Dorothy" was registered in New Hampshire during July, "that our growing business in this department may be protected." It wasn't until two years later, however, in 1903 (five years after Durgin's death), that the Canterbury Journal reports, "'The Dorothy' a trademark is registered in Washington, which protects us for 30 years in U.S. and all foreign countries."[22] The cloak was, in fact, trademarked as "Hart & Shepard," for Shaker Sisters Emmeline Hart (1834–1914) and Lucy Shepard (1836–1926), who were highly influential in the development of the industry.[23]

These matters, it seems, took time, but the result was more than satisfactory and long overdue for an industry that had been important in supporting that Community's economy since the late 1880s. This compelled their Sisters to spend an increasing number of days at their sewing machines filling orders. While early cloaks were made from cloth woven by the Shakers, as demand grew and production increased, they switched to a fine broadcloth imported from France.[24]

Dorothy Cape, child's (two views)
Wool and silk.
23½" l.; Early 20ᵗʰ C.
Canterbury Shaker Village, NH
Hancock Shaker Village, MA

The sizing of The Dorothy ranged from doll-sized to adult, with a full line for children, called "capes" when made without hoods. There were also versions made for infants, from six months to a year in age, which came in pink, white, and blue wool. These small cloaks sold for $5 in 1920.[25] In 1950, cloaks made for children aged two- to four-years-old sold for $7, for five- and six-year-olds, $8; and so on, up to $12 for the ten- to twelve-year-old set. It would appear cloaks for children were not exclusive to Canterbury, as Sister Anna Greaves of Mount Lebanon mentions completing an infant's cloak in her 1904 journal entry (see page 63).

Dorothy Cape, child's
Wool and silk.
23" l.; 1948.
Canterbury Shaker Village, NH
Shaker Museum | Mount Lebanon, NY

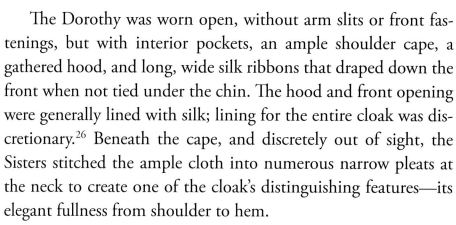

The Dorothy was worn open, without arm slits or front fastenings, but with interior pockets, an ample shoulder cape, a gathered hood, and long, wide silk ribbons that draped down the front when not tied under the chin. The hood and front opening were generally lined with silk; lining for the entire cloak was discretionary.[26] Beneath the cape, and discretely out of sight, the Sisters stitched the ample cloth into numerous narrow pleats at the neck to create one of the cloak's distinguishing features—its elegant fullness from shoulder to hem.

A 1900 order blank from East Canterbury, sent out to customers along with a small cameo portrait of Eldress Durgin, assures prospective buyers of the "Quality of materials and workmanship guaranteed to give satisfaction," and offers "different styles of finish" including "silk lined hood ribbons, cloaks with fronts silk lined, cloaks silk lined throughout. Made in two-thirds or full length the latter best for showing the gracefulness of the wrap."[27] Customers might choose from among the material swatches provided with the order form or supply their own fabric. They were asked to provide measurements for neck, shoulders, and length. Cloaks for adults required four yards of fifty-six-inch-wide cloth plus thirty inches of silk for the hood, and eleven yards of silk "of ordinary width" for a full lining.[28]

Dorothy Cloak (two views)
Wool and brocaded silk.
48" l.; Early 20th C.
Canterbury Shaker Village, NH
Canterbury Shaker Village, NH

Like their Mount Lebanon counterparts, at the turn of the century, the Canterbury Shaker Sisters were kept busy making cloaks (aka "opera cloaks") to meet the rising demand:

1900
Feb. 7 *Display of opera cloaks in Deaconesses room.* **Feb. 11** *Several orders for cloaks.* **Feb. 12** *Thirty-six opera cloaks made for sale during the past six weeks average $20 per cloak.* **Feb. 26** *To Franklin Falls SF Wilson, Blanch Gardines, Lillian Phelps to purchase goods for opera cloaks.* **Dec. 15** *Another week has passed with no abatement of demands for opera cloaks and sweaters. Opera cloaks and sweaters have been constantly ordered. The sisters have worked almost day and night to supply the various firms where sweaters are sold.* **Aug. 26** *Increasing demand for opera cloaks.*[29]

When the Sisters exhibited their cloaks along with other fancy goods at the Shoreham Hotel in Washington, D.C., the event was significant enough to warrant an announcement in the *Evening Star* newspaper: "A party of members of the Shaker community of East Canterbury, New Hampshire, are at the Shoreham Hotel, and since Monday have been giving exhibitions of the 'Dorothy' or Shaker cloaks and other holiday goods. The exhibition will continue until tomorrow."[30]

The Shaker Sisters from East Canterbury, N. H., will hold an Exhibition and Sale of Shaker Cloaks and Holiday Goods at

Hotel Brunswick, Copley Square, Boston
November 29 and 30, December 1, 2 and 3, 1910

107 Angell Street, Providence, R. I.
December 6, 7 and 8, 1910

Exhibit Open at 9 a. m.

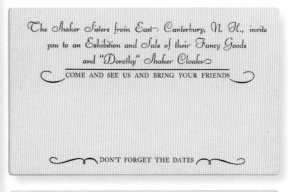

The Shaker Sisters from East Canterbury, N. H., invite you to an Exhibition and Sale of their Fancy Goods and "Dorothy" Shaker Cloaks
COME AND SEE US AND BRING YOUR FRIENDS
DON'T FORGET THE DATES

ESTEEMED FRIENDS:
YOU ARE KINDLY INVITED TO AN
Exhibition and Sale of Holiday Goods
And the "Dorothy" or Shaker Cloaks
By the Shaker Sisters from Enfield, New Hampshire, at

Postcard and Advertising Cards
Black ink on card paper,
5½" x 3½"; 1910.
5½" x 3¼"; Early 20th C.
Canterbury Shaker Village, NH
Communal Societies Collection,
Hamilton college, NY

The following year, on a day in late January, 1905, a Mr. Charles Hanf, from Victor, Achelis, & Co, in New York City "called at the [Canterbury] Village to consult with Hart & Shephard in regard to the broadcloth we are buying from this firm for 'Shaker Cloaks.' He remained only a few hours but his call was very satisfactory from a business standpoint."[31]

Ten years later, in 1915, a new opportunity for the Sisters to sell their cloaks through Filene's department store in Boston presented itself. In a departure from the usual practice of selling these by mail order or from the Sisters' fancy goods displays, Filene's made a tantalizing offer:

A new venture is to be tried on our Cloak business so announcement is made Feb. 7th. Filene and Sons [*sic*], Boston, ask permission to have their orders filled by us, for reselling in their store. Trustees agree to take a trial order and watch results, the cloaks to be paid upon the usual basis upon shipment.[32]

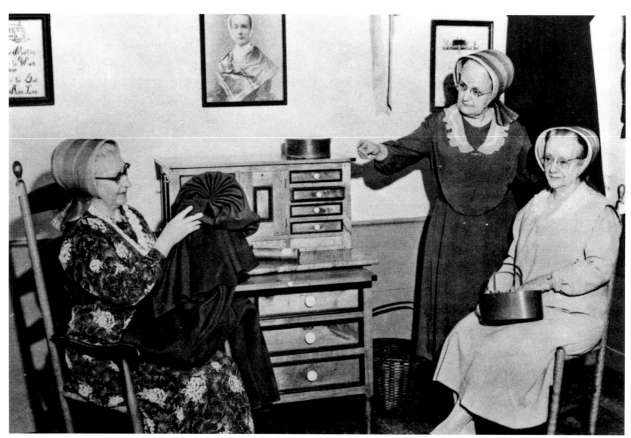

Photograph on card stock. 5½" x 3½"; ca. 1960. Srs. Bertha Lindsay and Miriam Wall (standing) with Sr. Lillian Phelps. Canterbury Shaker Village, NH Communal Societies Collection, Hamilton college, NY

Whether the collaboration with Filene's was successful or not is unknown, but the mere fact of its coming under discussion shows the impact on the World made by the stunning Shaker cloak. Filene's offer was a tribute to the Sisters' ingenuity, their exquisite attention to detail and styling, and their use of fine materials.

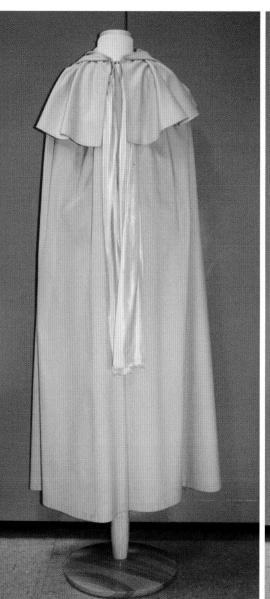

L.M. Noyes cloak (three views)
Wool and silk.
53¼" l.; Early 20th C.
Sabbathday Lake Shaker Village, ME
Shaker Museum | Mount Lebanon, NY

THE 1910 SABBATHDAY LAKE CATALOG opens with an enticing description of their Shaker cloak, drawing attention to the pinked seam edges:

> Enveloping the whole person, it falls in graceful folds to the hem of the dress, having a silk-lined hood for use in storms. Theses cloaks are made in many shades of the finest domestic and imported broadcloth. The latter is generally selected when one wishes a cloak lined throughout with silk. Such a garment is simply beautiful.
>
> The greatest care is exercised in the making of each cloak. All inner edges are prettily pinked, including the border of the pocket on each side of the garment.

Nearly all cloaks are made from the measurements of the individual, thus insuring a perfect fit. Samples of cloth in colors desired and silks for trimming or lining will be furnished on application, also blanks for giving orders.[33]

It was but nine years earlier that three Sabbathday Lake sisters traveled to Canterbury to learn the art of cloak-making. By mid-March, 1901, Eldress Lizzie Noyes was on her way to Boston to buy wool, and by April the new enterprise had begun.[34]

1901

Thursday, Jan. 25 *Elder Wm. Sarah J. and Amanda S. start for Canterbury. Sisters are going to learn to make old fashioned Shaker cloaks. There is a call for them all the time. They call them opera cloaks. So we shall have a new industry.*[35] **March 13** *Eldress Lizzie starts for Boston of first train. Will meet sister Lucy Ann Shephard there of Canterbury, NH. Together they will find cloth for cloaks.* **Fri. March 15** *Eldress Lizzie returns from Boston.* **Mon. April 8** *Sisters commence to make ladies cloaks for sale. A new industry and a promising one.*[36]

L.M. Noyes Cloak
Wool and silk.
47.5" l.; Early 20th C.
Sabbathday Lake
Shaker Village, ME
Hancock Shaker Village, MA

72

Several times a week during the summer, the Sabbathday Lake Sisters set up beautiful displays of their fancy goods and took orders for their cloaks at the nearby Poland Springs Hotel, then owned by the Ricker family. An accounting of the Sisters' activities around cloak-making shows they kept pace with mounting orders, making as many as ten or eleven cloaks a week. They used soft, pale colored wool in combination with a complementary silk lining, such as "the beautiful tan cloak lined with pink" mentioned on June 28.

[1901]
April Thurs. 18 *Sisters sell Shaker cloaks. This is the beginning.* **May 23** *Sarah and Amanda make two Shaker cloaks.* **Thurs. 30** *Sisters hurrying on cloaks, carriers, and dressing dolls.* **June 28** *Sisters make a beautiful tan cloak lined with pink, one that has been ordered.* **July 10** *Take three orders for cloaks besides selling one.* **July 12** *The Sisters have made a light cloak lined with lavender silk throughout for Mrs. Elliot one of the guests at the Poland Springs.* **Mon. July 29** *Vice President Hobarts [sic] wife Made a call. Nettie Ricker is measured for a cloak.* **Tues. July 30** *Nettie Ricker's cloak is finished and taken up to her.* **Aug. 6** *Ada went to the Springs with Eldress Elizabeth. . . took orders for five cloaks.* **Fri. 9** *Ada shortened a cloak for Mrs. Green with the aid of Cora Ricker's sewing machine.* **Sun. 18** *Sisters make 11 Shaker cloaks last week and still there are more orders.* **Wed. 21** *Ada and Elizabeth went to the Springs this evening. Ada brought home $96 for cloaks.* **Fri. 23** *Sisters have made 10 cloaks this week.* **Mon. 26** *Eldress Lizzie accompanied Ellen Stewart into Poland[, Maine,] then kept onto Boston to get goods for the cloaks.* **Sept. 7** *the Sisters have made 10 cloaks this week. Delmer Went to Lewiston and got a load of 100 boxes for cloaks.* **Dec.** *Sisters are making a cloak for Mrs. Brown of New York, Lined with silk throughout.*[37]

A year later, the Sisters— "working almost all the time"—barely kept up with the orders from hotel patrons:

July 14 *Eldress Lizzie went to Portland to get material for cloaks.* **Aug. 22** *Sisters have made three cloaks this week.* **Sept. 10 Wed.** *Sisters Sarah and Amanda are making a silk lined cloak for Mrs. Payne the Post Master General's wife.* **Sept. 12** *The Sisters make* *a beautiful white cloak for Mrs. Rogers lined throughout with silk.* **Oct. 14** *Sarah and Amanda working on cloaks about all the time. Orders keep coming from the Springs.*[38]

In October 1904 and 1906, according to the Sabbathday Lake Record, prices for a single cloak ranged between $20 and $35, depending on variations in lining and details. In July 1905, we find that "one cloak sold for as high as $53."[39] In 1910, customers paid $20 to $26 for cloaks made from domestic cloth and $30 to $33 for those of imported cloth. For cloaks with silk-lined shoulder capes the Shakers charged $3 extra; for one front faced with one width of silk, $7 extra; and for another silk-lined throughout, $16 extra.[40]

Pricing appears somewhat discretionary. Yet, when Elder Henry Green (1844-1931) of Alfred, Maine, wrote to apologize to Sister Clarissa of Mount Lebanon for underselling a cloak for $20 in 1902, his letter strikes a contrite note; he even offers to pay the difference out of his own pocket between the cloak's worth and what he sold it for:

> The amount received was for $46.00 for the two cloaks. I got full price for the tan and sold the red for $20. Because it was soiled and wrinkled badly. If I did wrong in selling so cheap you ought to charge me.[41]

FINAL DAYS OF SHAKER CLOAK SALES

THE CLOAK INDUSTRY faded from prominence after 1930. Why this happened has never been entirely clear, but women's styles had changed dramatically since the era of the Shaker cloak's greatest popularity at the turn of the century. As noted earlier, since 1915, sales suffered a gradual but steady decline. In part, this must have been a reaction to changing styles of dress during these crucial years of the First World War, the women's suffrage movement, and finally the Great Depression of October 1929. The drop-waisted, loose fitting flapper dresses of the twenties had given way to the trimmer, high-waisted, longer dresses and fitted coats of the thirties, when trousers for certain pastimes were considered *comme il faut*— proper or acceptable for women. The "liberated woman" of the thirties was less likely to want to be hampered by a cloak swirling around her ankles, restricting freedom of movement with an excess of cloth, and not nearly so practical as a coat for keeping out the weather. Eveningwear for the well-heeled fashion-conscious woman then included fur-embellished coats, stoles, wraps, and accessories.

Another factor for many was that money was tight in these years, when it was more common for a woman to remake old clothes than it was for her to buy new. Meanwhile, "new" to the clothing industry in the early days of mass production, as today, meant ready-to-wear, and not just for the woman on a budget.

Still, sources reveal an enduring, though far scarcer, enthusiastic following for Shaker cloaks into the mid-twentieth century. In 1930, for example, a note in the Canterbury records reads: "Jan. 7 M.A. Wilson [Eldress Mary Ann] and B.L. Phelps [Sister Bertha Lillian] to Florida and other southern resorts to sell cloaks and fancy goods. Home April 6th." In November 1933, we find this description presumably concerning a cloak made to order: "Black Dorothy cloak lined entirely with purple satin $36.00." [42] More poignant, as late as 1948, a letter from the Canterbury Shakers confirms the shipment of two children's cloaks to a customer: ". . . today Parcel Post Ins. a child's cloak in red, and a baby cape, to complete the samples previously sent to you. Trust they will be satisfactory in every way," followed by this pointed reference to marketing the cloaks: "We appreciate your kindness in trying to help us to a market for our work."[43]

By mid-century, a Shaker cloak was a treasured possession whose provenance was meticulously recorded and updated as the cloak changed hands several times before finding its way into a museum or private collection. For instance, the "beautiful medium dark red cloak" with a hood lined in purplish-red silk made before 1917 by Sister Emma J. Neale of Mount Lebanon for a Mrs. Cheeney of Pittsfield, Massachusetts, was subsequently purchased in 1955 from a woman in Ohio who had in turn bought it from Sister Jennie Wells, of Hancock Shaker Village. The cloak, as noted on the accession card at the Shaker Museum in Mount Lebanon, was "in fine condition" but for a few moth holes. Listed among those cloaks bought and sold several times is the one originally made for Mrs. Grover Cleveland then hastily replaced when found to have "a small spot on the front (which is still there)." This very cloak was bought in 1957 by a woman in Lee, Massachusetts, whose husband was raised by the Mount Lebanon Shakers. The cloak, which was never worn, has now come full circle, the cloak, returning to Mount Lebanon where it now resides in the Shaker Museum.[44]

Shaker cloaks represent the epitome of the fancy goods industry: ardently pursued and promoted by the Sisters of these three communities, as well as other New England Villages including Hancock, in Pittsfield, Massachusetts: Enfield, New Hampshire; and Alfred, Maine. The cloak's thoughtful design (with details characteristic of each Village), executed with meticulous care, and thoughtfully marketed (through print media and displays on site) met with enthusiasm from a World overtaken by an increasingly dominant manufacturing economy. Such finely fashioned, labor-intensive clothing would soon largely vanish from the marketplace, leaving the public all the poorer.

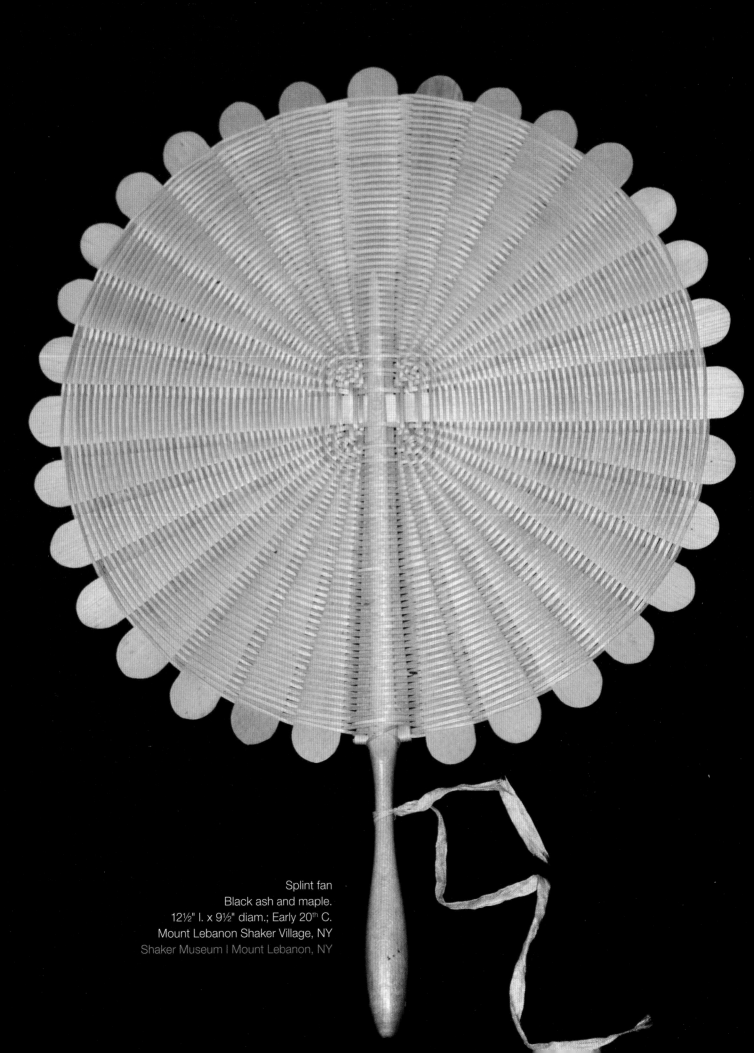

Splint fan
Black ash and maple.
12½" l. x 9½" diam.; Early 20th C.
Mount Lebanon Shaker Village, NY
Shaker Museum I Mount Lebanon, NY

7
SHAKER FANS

*Eighty-nine turkeys were plucked and prepared for market
in the Alfred, Maine, community in December 1878,
providing enough material for hundreds of fans.*[1]

FANS HAVE A LONG AND COLORFUL HISTORY as objects of practical and ceremonial use dating back to ancient Egypt—Tutankhamen was buried with eight—and the Middle Ages. In the European Middle Ages, fans, long associated with a gestural language of coquetry, were made of peacock, ostrich, parrot, or pheasant feathers, fixed into a mount of gold or silver and worn attached to the waist by a fine gold chain.[2] In the nineteenth century they became fashion accessories redolent of romance, mystery, wealth, and social position.[3] In the United States at that time, fans (fixed or folding) became mandatory for the stylishly attired woman; beautiful and useful, as always, to protect against the sun's glare and to generate cooling breezes.

For the Shakers, fans were objects of utility—meaning they were salable to the women of the World. They had none of the associations with wealth, romantic intrigue, art, and fashion that they had possessed in Europe and the Far East for centuries. Even so, by the late 1820s, the Shaker Sisters, canny about fashion trends and decades later attuned to the tastes and requirements of the new middle class, began making fixed fans of palm leaf to sell to the World. The first mention of fans occurs in a tally of objects in the Trustees [Gift] Store at New Lebanon, New York, in 1827: "Fancy goods such as—needlework, basketry, table, mats, fans. . ."[4] In July 1828, a journal from the Harvard Shakers reads: "two women from the Shirley South family walked to the local dry goods store and sold the proprietor three hats, two dozen fans, and some thread."[5] Records do not indicate

Photo
Sisters in North Family Gift Store
Photograph on paper.
7¼" x 4¼"; Late 19ᵗʰ C.
North Family, Mount Lebanon Shaker Village, NY
Communal Societies Collection, Hamilton college, NY

Palm fans (three)
Palm leaf.
14½" l. x 11"; 19th C.
Probably Shirley Shaker Village, Shirley, MA
Shirley Historical Society, MA

what type of fans these were but we know that the New England Shaker Sisters made fixed fans of turkey feathers (brown, black, and less commonly white), sometimes adorned with peacock feathers for a touch of the exotic, along with ones made of woven poplar and black ash, palm leaf, and folded paper. These paper fans opened in a full circle around the length of the handles in a style known as "cockade."

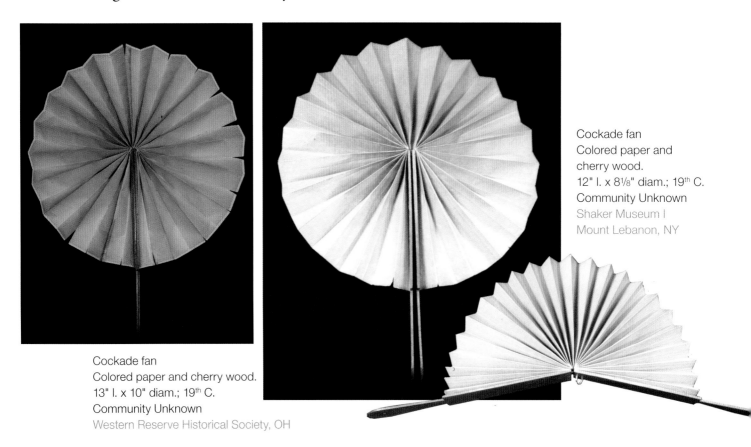

Cockade fan
Colored paper and
cherry wood.
12" l. x 8⅛" diam.; 19th C.
Community Unknown
Shaker Museum I
Mount Lebanon, NY

Cockade fan
Colored paper and cherry wood.
13" l. x 10" diam.; 19th C.
Community Unknown
Western Reserve Historical Society, OH

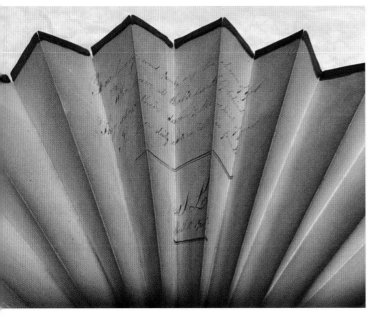

Cockade fan with a poem
"How lovely & pure are the chosen of God/ Who leave all that's earthly behind/ They show their descent, the spirit of good/ In their daily example is found. / S.L. April 12, 1832."
Colored paper and cherry wood. Photos by Danielle Peck.
Dimensions not recorded, 1832.
Community Unknown
Western Reserve Historical Society, OH

Cockade fan
Colored paper and cherry wood.
14" l. x 10½" diam.; 19th C.
Community Unknown
Shaker Museum I Mount Lebanon, NY

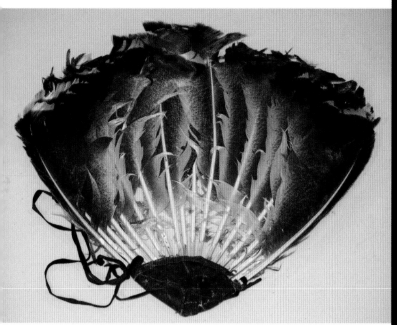

Turkey Feather Fan
Turkey feathers, ribbon, and leather.
14" x 15"; Mid. 19th C.
Possibly Shirley Shaker Village, MA
Shirley Historical Society, MA

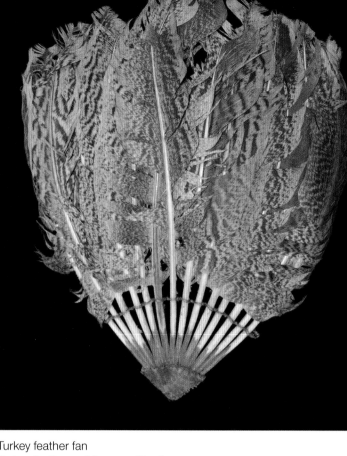

Turkey feather fan
Turkey feathers, ribbon, and leather.
12" x 9"; Mid-Late 19th C.
Probably Harvard Shaker Village, MA
Harvard Historical Society, MA

Between the 1870s and 1880s, the heyday for Shaker fans among women of the World, thousands of fans made with turkey feathers were produced at Sabbathday Lake.[6] According to New Lebanon Church Family records, they too produced fans by the thousands each year: 4,000 both in 1848 and in 1849.[7] Harvard records show a similar output.

Turkey Feather Fan
Turkey feathers and ribbon.
13" x 13"; Mid-Late 19th C.
Probably Harvard Shaker Village, MA
Harvard Historical Society, MA

South Family Barn. Photograph on paper, 12" x 8"; 1940. Harvard Shaker Village, MA Private Collection

Indeed, the fan-making industry, common to most New England Shaker Communities, proved to be so lucrative to the Harvard Shaker Village that it supported the building of a new cow barn there. As Clara Endicott Sears (1863-1960) observed in *Gleanings from Old Shaker Journals*, "The large and handsome Stone [cow] Barn at the South Family [in Harvard] . . . was built with money earned in making the then popular turkey feather fans."* In a gesture of generosity, offering further proof of the large profits also made from the fan-making industry at the Canterbury Community, on October 21, 1835, "Br True W. Heath [of Canterbury] came here [Harvard] and brought 10,000 shingles for the South Family's new stone barn. 20,000 more are on their way here, these are given *gratis*."[8] In 1853, when a fire destroyed this same cow barn, the Sabbathday Lake Sisters offered the profits from the sale of their turkey feather fans to support its rebuilding.[9]

References to the Harvard fan industry abound in the journals of Elder Grove Blanchard (1797-1880). On November 29, 1836, Elder Blanchard writes, "Tuesday, sky overcast, and weather cold, Grove ties 15 dozen fans. . . ,"[10] then, on January 10, 1837, he notes, "Grove ties fans...Seth and Betsy here about fan business. . . they conclude to sell them at $92 per 100 dozen, as counseled from Lebanon."[11]

* Clara Endicott Sears, comp., *Gleaning From Old Shaker Journals* (Boston: Houghton Mifflin,1916), 222-223.

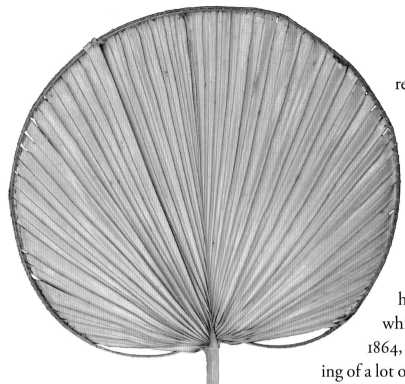

Palm fan
Palm leaf.
14½" l. x 10" diam.; 19th C.
Probably Harvard
Shaker Village, MA
Harvard Historical Society, MA

Elder Blanchard's journals continue to record his daily fan production: May 8, 1838, "Tuesday, some showers, some fair, Grove ties fans. . ."[12] The next day, May 9, Wednesday, "Fair – with showers, Grove finish tying fans; Olive B, and Almira Adams help me do some turkey feather fans in the PM. . ."[13] According to the Harvard Shaker Journals, on Monday, September 29, 1845: "Dennis Pratt came here [Harvard] and paid for 92 ½ doz. Fans which amounted to $38.85."[14] On July 27, 1864, Elder Blanchard writes: "I finish the sewing of a lot of palm leaf fans, have sewed a batch of mats & fans, say 70 or 75 sets of mats and 6 dozen fans."[15] (By this time, the Civil War had disrupted shipments of palm leaf from Cuba and the Caribbean, so it's likely the Shakers purchased palm leaf from Italy and Africa at the Port of Boston.[16])

The process for making fans was fairly simple, allowing for rapid production during the mid-nineteenth century when carrying a fan was de rigueur among women of all classes. During November and December, or "picking time" as they called it, the Shaker Brothers and Sisters would gather turkey feathers and down. At the Harvard Shaker Village, a brick oven in one of the houses was used to steam the turkey feathers into the curved shape necessary for the fan-making. The feathers were held in place with rosettes of cloth or leather in varying styles.

Fans of black ash or poplar were occasionally woven on the loom as placemats were, and indeed some of these fans appear to have been made of two such "mats" stitched back to back. Fans of woven fibers had either slender twigs or turned maple sticks for handles. Woven palm leaf fans consisted of a single leaf whose fibers had been stripped and woven "with the wrapped stalk forming [the] handle."[17] The Sisters and Brothers made cockade fans of paper, often dyed in soft earth tones, as well as bright yellow and blue. Their handles consisted of two paddle-shaped sticks of thin wood, or occasionally wood turned on a lathe by Shaker Brethren. Silk ribbons were sometimes threaded through a hole at the end of the handle for suspending from the wearer's wrist. ——

Materially modest but stylish, Shaker fans combined transcendent simplicity with meticulous handwork. Sisters and Brothers were equally engaged in the industry. They sold surprisingly well, providing the Shaker Communities with a substantial stream of income. Furthermore, unlike the related industry of poplarware box production that was very labor intensive, fans could be made with relative ease, using mostly locally available materials (with the exception of palm leaf). Fans embodied the Shakers' special sense of beauty, proportion, utility—and salability.

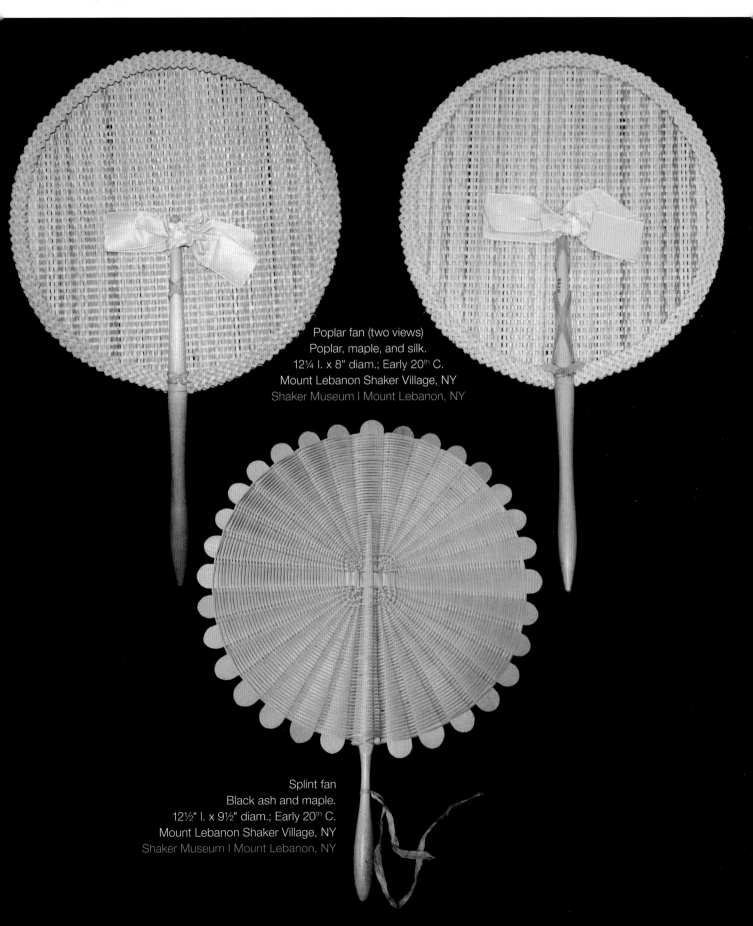

Poplar fan (two views)
Poplar, maple, and silk.
12¼" l. x 8" diam.; Early 20ᵗʰ C.
Mount Lebanon Shaker Village, NY

Splint fan
Black ash and maple.
12½" l. x 9½" diam.; Early 20ᵗʰ C.
Mount Lebanon Shaker Village, NY

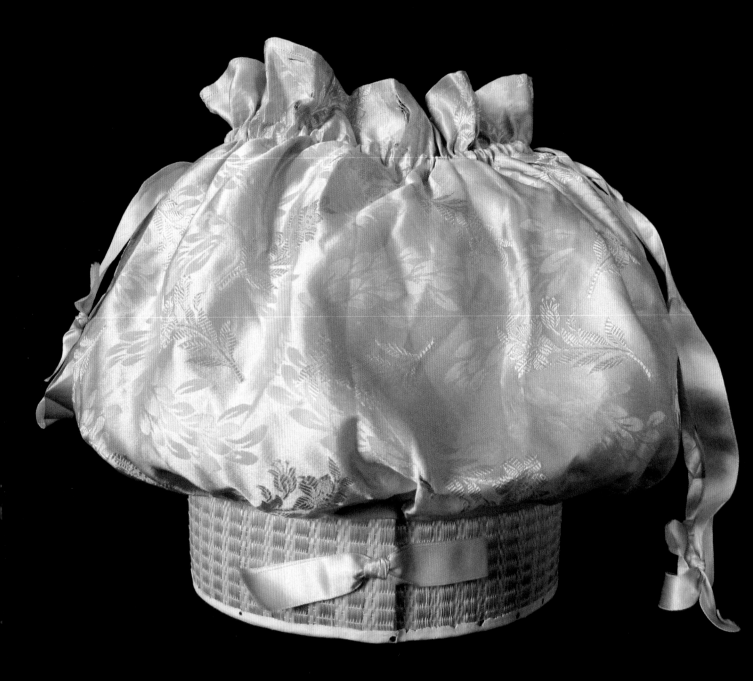

Sewing Bag
Poplar cloth, silk, and kid leather.
7¼" x 2¼"; Late 19th C.
Enfield Shaker Village, NH
Enfield Shaker Museum, NH

POPLARWARE BOXES

Oct. 24 1894 *Sister Aurelia* [Mace] *has beamed a web of 100 yards of thread for weaving poplar for the sisters* [*sic*] *basket work.*[1]

THE SISTERS BEGAN MAKING ORANGE-PEEL BOXES at Canterbury, New Hampshire. In 1843, Shakers there listed paper-covered orange peel boxes for sale among other fancy goods items.[2] Cardboard boxes were covered with decorative papers of various kinds, including marbleized, silvered, patterned, and wood-grained, as early as the 1840s. These early boxes, their interiors lined with brightly colored cloth or velvet, and in some cases fitted-out with pincushions, served as prototypes for the more intricate, ambitious, and handsome poplarware that followed.[3] By the time the poplarware industry reached its peak in the early twentieth century, boxes covered in woven poplar cloth were making a substantial contribution to the Shakers' economy.

Orange Peel Box
Orange peel and paper.
2¼" x 1⅝"; 1847.
Canterbury Shaker Village, NH
Hancock Shaker Village, MA

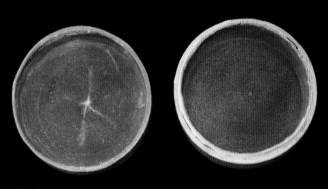

Interior of Orange Peel Box.

Orange Peel Box
Orange peel and paper.
.25c written on bottom of box,
3¼" x 1½"; 1870.
Canterbury Shaker Village, NH
Western Reserve Historical Society, OH

Orange Peel Box
Orange peel and paper.
3½" x 2⅝" diam.; Second half of 19th C.
Canterbury Shaker Village, NH
Shaker Museum I Mount Lebanon, NY

While it is speculated that this industry originated at various Shaker Villages, the production of poplarware grew out of the earlier market for cardboard boxes. Furthermore, it is a fact that the first Village to undertake its large-scale production was New Lebanon, New York. Their poplarware appears to have derived from the black ash basket industry, an example of which is shown below:

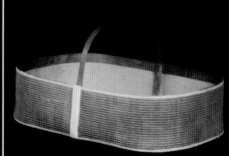

Black Ash Basket, 12¾" h x 20⅝" w x 14⅛" d. black ash basket, 8½" h x 13" w x 9½" d. poplar with Homespun Cloth Covering, 10½" h x 19⅞" w x 18⅜" d.

For close to a century, from 1860 and 1958, the poplarware industry—original and unique to the Shakers—helped significantly in supporting the New England and New York Shaker Communities. By 1855, the Shaker Sisters, always resourceful in their use of readily available materials, began to weave cloths using rye, oat, straw, grass, and imported palm leaf for hats, fans, and table mats on looms warped with cotton thread.[4] Around 1858, the New Lebanon Sisters added poplar strips to their fans, and in 1860, Deaconess Betsy

Crosman (1804–1892) "recorded in her journal having made thirty small "popple" (as the Shakers called poplar) covered baskets for sale."[5] By 1861, when the Community changed its name to Mount Lebanon, the Sisters started weaving poplar cloth ("popple web") for their fancy baskets as a handsome and practical alternative to palm leaf.[6] Cardboard or wood boxes, covered in poplar cloth, in geometric shapes, meticulously crafted, and designed to store mainly sewing accessories, soon followed.[7] These were generally lined with silk (in a satin weave) and adorned with ribbons, both decorative and functional.

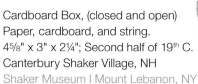

Cardboard Box, (closed and open)
Paper, cardboard, and string.
4⅝" x 3" x 2¼"; Second half of 19th C.
Canterbury Shaker Village, NH
Shaker Museum I Mount Lebanon, NY

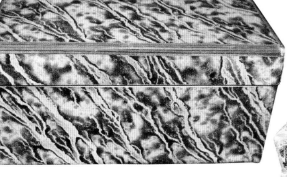

Cardboard Box
Paper, cardboard, and wood.
4" x 3" x 2¼"; Second half of 19th C.
Canterbury Shaker Village, NH
Shaker Museum I Mount Lebanon, NY

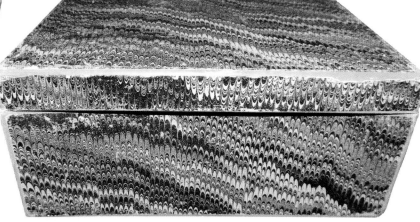

Cardboard Box
Paper and cardboard.
7" x 4½" x 3"; Second half of 19th C.
Canterbury Shaker Village, NH
Shaker Museum I Mount Lebanon, NY

Cardboard Box
Paper and cardboard.
6¼" x 4¼" x 2½": Second half 19th C.
Hancock Shaker Village, MA
Shaker Museum | Mount Lebanon, NY

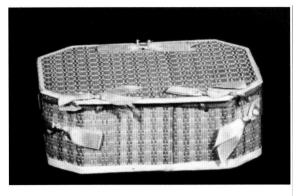

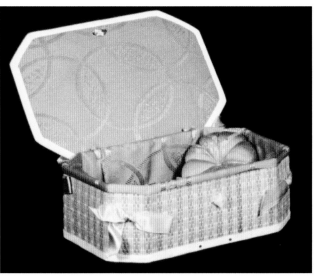

Work Box
Poplar cloth, silk, and kid leather.
6¼" x 4" x 2¾"; Early 20ᵗʰ C.
North Family, Mount Lebanon Shaker Village, NY
Private Collection

New Lebanon's Sisters continued to weave palm-leaf fibers as well as poplar into cloth until 1861, when the Civil War disrupted shipments of palm from Cuba and the Caribbean. They turned then to poplar, a soft wood that had limited use in furniture making, did not burn well, yet grew in abundance, as a readily available replacement. Another reason for discontinuing palm leaf cloth was the difficulty of stripping, gauging, and weaving the two palm "threads," as well as drying and "bleaching" the fiber (in burning sulfur fumes) to remove their natural green tinge.[8] The Sabbathday Lake Shakers took up the art of weaving and working with poplar cloth in 1863, when Elder Otis Sawyer (1815–1884) brought back examples of poplarware, as well as the knowledge of their manufacture, from Mount Lebanon. He then produced the first poplar strips suitable for being loom-woven.[9] Shortly thereafter, Elder William Dumont (1851–1930) learned the trade and eventually took charge of the work at Sabbathday Lake until his death in 1930.

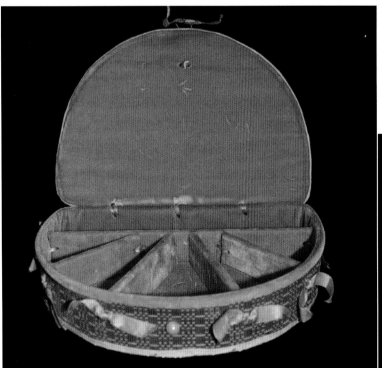

Ladies' Jewel Box (open and closed)
Poplar cloth, velvet, silk, elastic, button, and kid leather.
8¾" x 6" x 1¾"; ca. 1900.
Sabbathday Lake Shaker Village, ME
Western Reserve Historical Society, OH

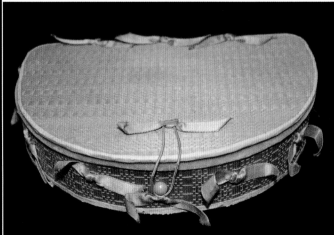

The Canterbury Community began making poplarware in 1893.[10] The multifaceted poplarware industry there became a Community endeavor, drawing on the Sisters' combined skills of weaving, basket making, and sewing, along with the Brothers' facility for cutting and splitting the poplar trees. They eventually designed a steam engine for stripping the poplar.[11] Preparing the poplar strips, weaving the cloth, and fashioning it into boxes took place in the winter, with the boxes completed before spring planting when other chores took precedence. "The first step was the careful selection and cutting of the trees, which had to be from moist land," wrote Sabbathday Lake Sister Elsie McCool (1900–1993), in The Shaker Quarterly.[12] There is evidence that at times the Shakers paid for their poplar wood as these Mount Lebanon Journal entries show: March 8 1869 Paid for popple lumber [$] 21.00; Sept. 20 1872 Paid for Sewing Lumber at Adamses [sic] Mill.[13] Sometimes, too, nature had a hand in the annual poplar tree harvest: Mon June 4 Brethren finish peeling the bark from 30 trees which were blown down from the great storm last November. The logs will now be in good condition to be hauled home next winter.[14]

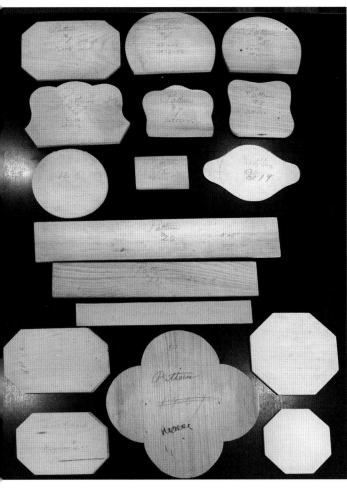

Poplarware Forms
Various sizes.
Canterbury Shaker Village, NH
Private Collection

Poplarware
Woven poplar cloth strips used in making poplarware boxes and patterns.
Canterbury Shaker Village, NH
Private Collection

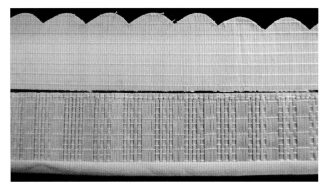

Poplarware strips
Poplar cloth trimmed with kid leather.
Top: Mount Lebanon Shaker Village, NY
Bottom: Canterbury Shaker Village, NH
Private Collection

The Poplar Process

The following photos were assembled in a photo album by
Sister Bertha Lindsay of Canterbury Shaker Village, NH, 1950

Shaker Museum | Mount Lebanon, NY

Hauling poplar logs

Standing trees

Planing the poplar

Spreading the poplar to dry

Shredding the poplar

Spool frame, putting on warp

Poplar loom

Sister at work at the poplar loom

Woven poplar cloth and strips

Sister using stiletto for making holes

Sisters tacking
poplar to bases

Sister tying on cover
of poplar box

Canterbury, NH,
poplar box display

For the first step in the time- and labor-intensive process of producing poplarware, Brethren brought poplar tree trunks to the mill where they were cut into twenty-four inch lengths. After the bark was removed, each log was split into eighths, producing sticks or blocks two to two-and-one-half inches square. The poplar logs, kept frozen to produce smoother shavings, were planed by hand into strips one-sixteenth of an inch thick.[15] Now the Sisters stepped in to dry and straighten the curled poplar strips using flat irons. Sister Elsie McCool gives a vivid account of the setup and the ensuing work:

> One side of the room in which the planer was located contained a long table set up temporarily for the processing of the shavings. Several sisters seated around it would straighten each piece of poplar by quickly drawing it between the index and middle fingers of the right hand. Care had to be taken to have all cham-fered ends (a 45-degree angle cut along with the grain) at the top and each strip laid right side down, as there was a right and wrong side to each piece. The strips were stacked into large baskets and taken from the sawmill to the laun-dry. It was still necessary to store them where they might be kept frozen. The next step in the process was the drying of the poplar. This was done in our large ironing room. The strips were spread around the room on large double racks on which the strips were repeatedly turned in the drying process. The intense heat of the room and the moisture from the frozen poplar soon produced a humidity which quickly exhausted the sisters engaged in the work. Several sisters worked in this department and had to take great care that the strips dried flat and thoroughly.[16]

The laborious task of cutting the poplar strips by hand came to an end in 1872, when Brother Granville Merrill (1839–1878), an accomplished mechanic, designed and built a steam engine that, when combined with a gauging wheel, was used to slice the poplar into one-eighth-inch strips quickly and accurately. "It took three sisters to tend the gauge; one to pass, one to feed the gauge, and someone particularly quick to catch the finished strip," wrote McCool. "And still the strips had to be spread for drying and stored in a dark place to prevent the sun from darkening the wood fibers."[17]

The Sisters wove the cloth on looms wound with a warp of 216 30-gauge white cotton threads, through which they drew the poplar strands using a pair of long wooden tongs with sandpaper tips to hold the poplar securely. For variety, sweet grass was sometimes added to the poplar weft: "Thur. March 5 1896 Sister Ada [Cummings] is weaving sweet grass in with the poplar webbing for ladies' work baskets."[18] This practice continued but could not compete with the pure woven poplar for looks and popularity.

Once they had eleven or twelve yards of poplar cloth, the Sisters cut off ten yards from the loom, pasted plain white paper to the back to strengthen the cloth and prevent it from raveling. They covered the paper with white cloth that was ironed dry. Now, using a machine that resembled a present day paper cutter, they cut lengths and strips of poplar cloth according to a pattern determined by the size of the box. For example:

Jan. 1912 amount of poplar and satin needed in order to make product
    EX: Square 5" box
    Poplar strip 21½" long x 2½" wide
    Satin strip 22½" long x 3" wide.[19]

Handkerchief Box, (open and closed)
Poplar cloth, silk, elastic, button, and kid leather.
5" x 5' x 2¼"; Early 20th C.
Sabbathday Lake Shaker Village, ME
Private Collection

Sabbathday Lake Community records from the late nineteenth century give a good account of the early stages of the process, which took place over several seasons of poplar tree harvesting and gauging:

    [1895]
    Jan. 15 *Elder Wm. Got out poplar for sisters* [sic] *sale work.*
        Jan. 18 *Sisters commence on poplar sale work.* **Jan. 28** *Brother Henry Green arrived from Alfred. He is to assist from getting out the poplar shaving both from this place and from Alfred.* **Jan. 30** *Sisters straighten poplar at the mill.* **Feb. 1** *The poplar work at*

the mill is finished. 12 large baskets full. The sewing is put up at the mill for the present. **Feb. 4** *The little engine is set up in the washroom to gauge the poplar.* **Feb. 8** *Finish gauging the poplar this forenoon. Enough for three years elder Wm. Thinks.*[20]

[1901]
Jan. 1 *Elder Wm. Walked to Raymond [Maine] to find poplar trees for the fancy work.* **Jan. 2** *poplar trees cut and draw* [sic] *to the mill from Raymond wood.* **Feb. 6** *poplar all gauged, dried and put away.*[21]

Poplar suited the Shakers' purposes well. The trees (*liriodendron tulipifera*, a.k.a. American tulip, tulip poplar, or yellow poplar) grew throughout the Eastern United States. Poplar fibers were tensile, the sapwood an attractive creamy white, straight-grained, and of uniform texture.[22] Because strength was not one of its virtues, "Each box had a wooden foundation or bottom." The poplar cloth had to be reinforced with cardboard, both on the sides and on the lid. First the pieces were sewn together and then a strand of wire was sewn to the edge of the cardboard that formed the box. The satin-woven silk and wadding linings were stitched into the bottom, after which the frame was tacked onto the wooden foundation.[23]

Finished boxes. Canterbury, NH

Each fancy box went through eighteen processes, noted Sister McCool, before being considered complete. Each had matching silk ribbons sewn on to secure the lid and an elastic band to fasten it in front. The boxes might be outfitted with sewing accessories such as an emery, pincushion, needle book, and wax, or partitioned and lined with velvet for holding jewelry. Other boxes were meant for storing cuffs, collars, and gloves. "At the peak of box production, twenty-one different styles of boxes and baskets were made," wrote Sister McCool. By the early 1960s, when box production had dropped from close to five hundred a year to a mere handful, the number of styles at Sabbathday Lake had dwindled to six.[24]

Box shapes from the different Communities included oval, heart, square, hexagonal, demi-lunar, and rectangular; styles and decorative materials varied, as did the pattern of the poplar cloth weave. Today, the origin of the boxes can be determined in part by these variations in materials and weave patterns. For example, the Mount Lebanon Church Family generally used white dotted paper on the bottom of their boxes, most of which retained the wooden forms that they were made on, as did boxes from the Alfred Community. Sabbathday Lake boxes were removed from their wood forms and then covered with glossy papers on the bottom.

Canterbury experimented with contemporary fabrics and patterned papers on their box bottoms, seemingly using wallpaper samples. Canterbury also sold their poplarware in cardboard boxes, with "Manufactured by the Canterbury Shakers, East Canterbury, New Hampshire" printed on the top of each box. The poplarware produced at Alfred and Sabbathday Lake, after around 1903, was consistently distinguished by a stamp on the bottom of each piece that had been designed by Brother Delmer Wilson (1873–1961). Mount Lebanon and Canterbury poplarware was generally sold without a stamp or other distinguishing mark.[25]

Paper and cloth
Wallpaper pieces used for box bottoms and silk pieces.
Canterbury Shaker Village, NH
Private Collection

Each Community had a "signature" poplar weaving pattern with signature variations too. The Mount Lebanon Church Family made a flat weave pattern. The North Family there used grasses in their poplarware. Enfield, New Hampshire, at times, incorporated straw in their weaves. Alfred, Maine, incorporated sweet grass into its later poplarware. Additional materials, such as a heavy white tape to trim raw edges, was commonly used at Mount Lebanon, instead of the usual white kidskin, a practice that was sometimes employed on Sabbathday Lake boxes as well. Pincushions in poplar bases were called basket cushions or basket balls.[26]

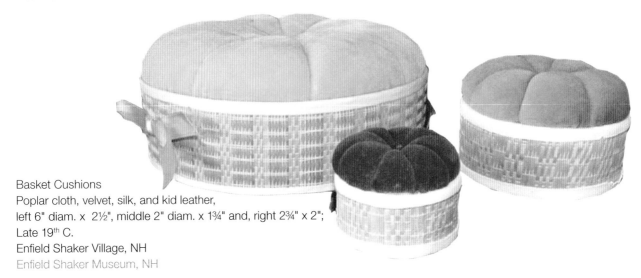

Basket Cushions
Poplar cloth, velvet, silk, and kid leather,
left 6" diam. x 2½", middle 2" diam. x 1¾" and, right 2¾" x 2";
Late 19th C.
Enfield Shaker Village, NH
Enfield Shaker Museum, NH

Each Community had a characteristic method of tying ribbons too, providing collectors with another clue to itsprovenance.[27] Poplar patterns are shown below. Colors vary due to oxidation and exposure of the poplar over time.

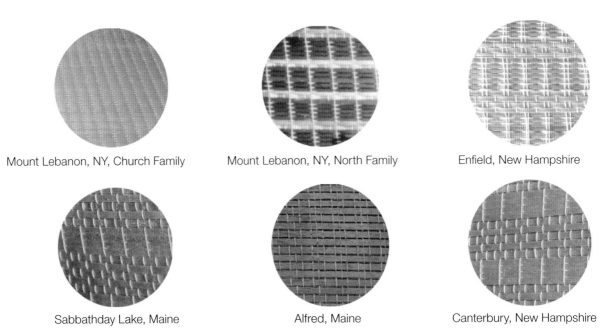

Mount Lebanon, NY, Church Family

Mount Lebanon, NY, North Family

Enfield, New Hampshire

Sabbathday Lake, Maine

Alfred, Maine

Canterbury, New Hampshire

A spirit of cooperation prevailed among the New York and New England Shaker Communities in this industry. When needs arose, they traded or purchased both raw materials and finished goods amongst them. In 1875, for example, following a devastating fire at Mount Lebanon, the Maine Societies offered their New York Sisters woven poplar cloth, finished work boxes, and specialty boxes for handkerchiefs, gloves, collars, and jewelry "so that they would not be without merchandise to sell."[28] The Mount Lebanon Journal reported in 1877 "poplar wove cloth for sale 10 yards."[29] In his 1905 account book, Sabbathday Lake Elder Otis Sawyer recorded: "purchasing poplar from Alfred [Maine]." And soon after: "For poplar Alfred, 16.40." That same year, he noted receiving for the sale of poplar, a "check from Canterbury poplar 10.50."[30]

In his essay, "Shaker Collecting," James Elliot—the pseudonym for Sabbathday Lake Brother Theodore Johnson (1930–1986)—reported that the Church Family at Mount Lebanon, New York, not only produced finished pieces of poplarware but also made poplar shavings that were used by the North Family there. He went on to say that these shavings were also cut on a machine made by Brother Delmer Wilson (1873–1961) at Sabbathday Lake, Maine. Throughout the history of the industry, more poplarware was produced at the Sabbathday Lake Community than at any other Shaker Village. According to Brother Ted Johnson, in addition to producing finished pieces, Sabbathday Lake also made the raw poplar strips for the Communities at Alfred, Maine, and at Canterbury and Enfield, New Hampshire.[31]

Small Box
Poplar, oat straw, silk, elastic, button, and kid leather.
Made by Sister Martha Wetherell
4¼" x 3¼" x 1¼", 1900
Canterbury Shaker Village, NH
Western Reserve Historical Society, OH

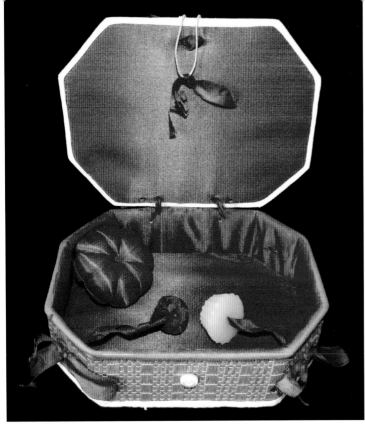

Octagon Box, (open and closed)
Poplar cloth, silk, emery, wax, elastic, button, and kid leather.
7¼" x 5" x 2¾"; Early 20th C
Canterbury Shaker Village, NH
Western Reserve Historical Society, OH

A penchant for sharing skills and knowledge, too, lies at the heart of many Shaker fancy goods endeavors. For example, Sister Martha Wetherell (1855–1944), who began her Shaker life at Mount Lebanon is credited for starting the poplarware trade at Canterbury and for incorporating hand-dyed poplar strips into their cloth. This is a decorative touch which distinguishes her boxes today.[32]

> **Oct. 30 1895** *Poplar Dying for fancy work by L.A.S, S.F.W &*
> *M.W.*[33]
> **Nov. 6 1896** *Lucy Ann & Co. engaged in dying goods and poplar*
> *for fancy work.*[34]

The Shakers sold their poplarware from their Village stores, in printed catalogs, displayed them in showrooms at resort hotels throughout New England and New York, and brought them on sales trips up and down the eastern seaboard. These trips took them to resorts as far south as Florida.[35] From the turn of the nineteenth century into the 1920s, these entries offer a snapshot of Sister Martha Wetherell's sales trips:

> **Dec. 4 1894** *Martha Wetherell and Julia Briggs go to Providence to*
> *sell goods.*
> **Dec. 12 [1894]** *The sisters return from Providence.*[36]
> **Feb. 27, 1900** *The Brooklyn Daily Eagle reports Sister Wetherell's*
> *arrival in New York for a sales trip; Hotel Arrivals, Clarendon,*

Mary L. Wilson, Martha Wetherell, East Canterbury, N.H."[37]

1913 July 21 *Martha Wetherell and Str. Angeline Brown start for Cape Cod on a business trip.*

1913 Aug. 17 *Sisters Martha Wetherell and Angeline Brown return from the cape* [sic].

1919 April 24 *Martha Wetherell leaves home for a trip to Boston.*

1919 May 11 *Martha Wetherell returns home from Boston.*

1922 Sep. 21 *Martha Wetherell, Laura [Beals] and Rosetta [Stephens] with four brethren attens* [sic] *the Eastern [States] Exposition, held at Springfield, Mass.*[38]

Between 1930 and 1950, the Canterbury Sisters produced poplar goods at the astonishing rate of close to 500 items per year. Between 1930 and 1940, for example, they made 4,736 pieces; in the following decade, 4,970 pieces. By the fifties, however, trade had slowed. While the Sisters there still made close to 3,000 boxes between 1950 and 1958, averaging 324 boxes a year, in the final year production dropped to a mere twenty-six boxes, anticipating the end of an era.[39]

The poplarware industry at Canterbury came to a halt in 1957–58 when one of the gauging machines was stolen. That year, Eldress Bertha Lindsay (1897–1990), who had taken charge of the poplar box trade in 1944, and Sister Flora Appleton (1881–1962), made the last suite of poplar boxes. These were a birthday gift for Charles "Bud" Thompson, the beloved curator of their museum.

At Sabbathday Lake, a blight killed off many poplars and the Great Mill there closed in 1942, making it impossible to process poplar logs.[40] Their Sisters, however, continued to make boxes covered with store-bought cloth and leatherette (a practice started in 1943) until 1958 when production stopped entirely.

At the peak of this vital industry, from around 1910 to 1940, poplarware boxes were an important source of income for the surviving Shaker communities of Mount Lebanon, Canterbury, Alfred, and Sabbathday Lake (although Alfred closed in 1931). Like many other fancy goods items, poplarware demanded full-on engagement, with every facet of production requiring patience, exactitude, and skill. It also required the skills of Brothers assisting Sisters. As the Brethren devised better and faster ways to prepare the poplar for weaving, the Sisters aligned their refined sense of ornamentation and insight with the changing fashions of the world in the design and details of their wares. Ultimately, a dwindling Shaker population, along with competition from cheaper goods that were sold at department stores and mall shops, brought the industry to a halt.

Square Box
Made by Sister Martha Wetherell
Poplar cloth and woven oat straw, silk,
elastic, button, and kid leather.
Approximately 5" x 5" x 2"; 1938.
North Family, Mount Lebanon, NY
Hancock Shaker Village, MA

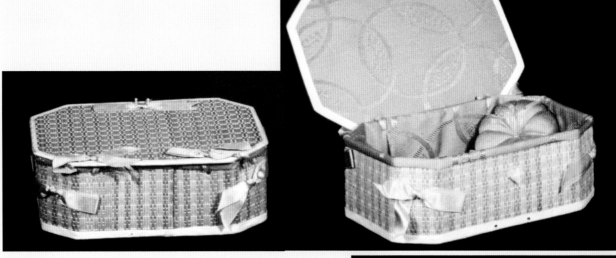

Work Box
Poplar cloth, silk, and kid leather.
6¼" x 4" x 2¾"; Late 19th C.
North Family, Mount Lebanon Shaker Village, NY
Private Collection

Mount Lebanon stamp
6¼" x 4" x 2¾"; Late 19th C.
North Family, Mount Lebanon Shaker Village, NY
Private Collection

North Family

Work Box, (open and closed)
Poplar cloth, silk, emery, wax, and kid leather.
7 3/8" x 5 "x 2¾"; Late 19th C.
North Family, Mount Lebanon Shaker Village, NY
Private Collection

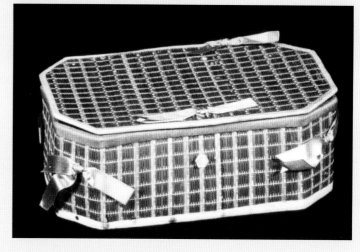

Postcard
North Family Store
5½' x 3½"; Late 19th C.
North Family, Mount Lebanon
Shaker Village, NY
Private Collection

Catalog
Products of Intelligence
and Diligence
7" x 4⅝"; 1908.
Private Collection

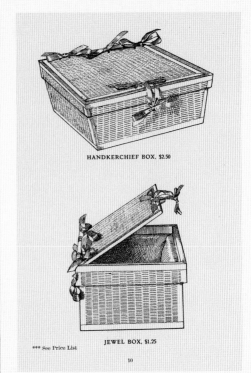

Catalog
Detail.

Jewel Box
Poplar cloth, silk, emery, and kid leather.
5" x 5" x 2½"; Late 19th C.
Church Family, Mount Lebanon Shaker Village, NY
Shaker Museum I Mount Lebanon, NY

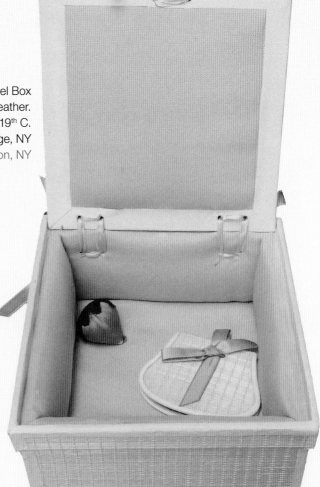

Church Family

Square Work Box. Poplar cloth and paper tape, 3" x 3" x 2½"; Late 19th C. Church Family, Mount Lebanon Shaker Village, NY

Jewel Box
Poplar wood, silk, and paper tape.
4¼" x 4¼" x 2¼"; Late 19th C.
Church Family, Mount Lebanon Shaker Village, NY

Jewel Box Form
Poplar wood.
3⅝" x 3⅝" x 2⅛"; Late 19th C.
Church Family, Mount Lebanon Shaker Village, NY

Mount Lebanon, NY

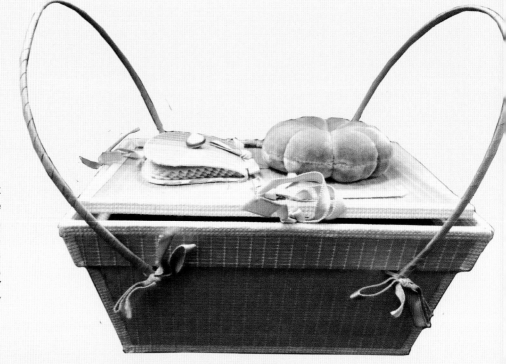

Oblong Work Box
Poplar cloth, velvet, silk, poplar needle
book, poplar wrapped handles,
and kid leather.
6¼" x 4½" x 2¾"; Late 19th C.
Church Family,
Mount Lebanon Shaker Village, NY
Shaker Museum I Mount Lebanon, NY

Oblong Work Box
Poplar cloth, silk, black ash,
velvet, felt, poplar wrapped
handles, and paper tape.
9⅛" x 5⅜" x 4"; Late 19th C.
Church Family, Mount
Lebanon Shaker Village, NY
Private Collection

Church Family

Oval Work Stand
Poplar cloth, velvet, silk, black ash, poplar wood, and kid leather.
9" x 5⅜" x 2⅝"; Late 19th C.
Church Family, Mount Lebanon Shaker Family, NY
Private Collection

Heart-Shaped Box
Poplar cloth, black ash, velvet, wool, paper, and kid leather.
6¼" x 6" x 2¼"; 1890–1930.
Church Family, Mount Lebanon Shaker Village, NY
Shaker Museum I Mount Lebanon, NY

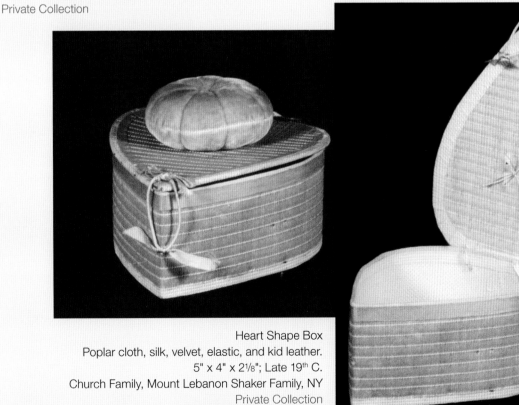

Heart Shape Box
Poplar cloth, silk, velvet, elastic, and kid leather.
5" x 4" x 2⅛"; Late 19th C.
Church Family, Mount Lebanon Shaker Family, NY
Private Collection

Drawer Box
Poplar cloth, silk, velvet, black ash, poplar wrapped handle, and kid leather.
7½" x 6" x 3½"; Late 19th C.
Church Family, Mount Lebanon Shaker Family, NY
Private Collection

Work Box
Poplar cloth, poplar wood, silk, and tape.
3½" x 3½" x 2"; 1880–1900.
Church family, Mount Lebanon, NY
Western Reserve Historical Society, OH

Diamond-Shaped Basket
Poplar cloth, silk, and poplar wrapped handle.
3⅜" x 3".; Late 19th C.
Church Family, Mount Lebanon Shaker Village, NY
Private Collection

Polly Lewis South Family store Mount Lebanon.
Stereo-view photograph on stiff cardboard.
Card 7" x 3½"; image 3" x 3"; 1870.
Sister Polly Lewis in South Family Gift Shop.
Mount Lebanon Shaker Village, NY
Private Collection

Basket Cushions
Poplar cloth, velvet, silk, and kid leather,
left 6" diam. x 2½", middle 2" diam. x 1¾" and, right 2¾" diam. x 2"; Late 19th C.
Enfield Shaker Village, NH
Enfield Shaker Museum, NH

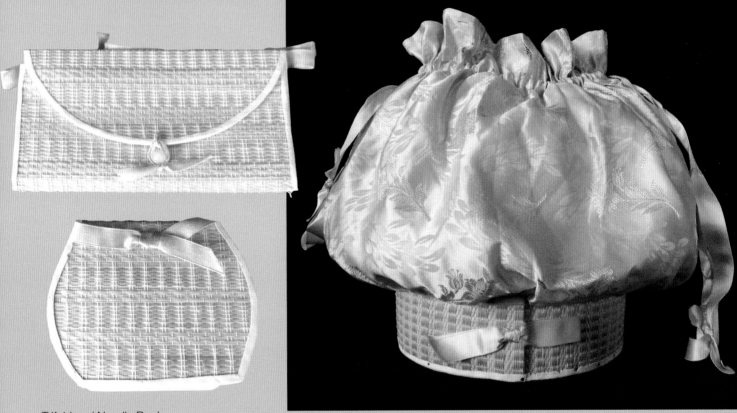

Trifold and Needle Book
Top: poplar cloth, silk, elastic, button, and kid leather.
4 ½" x 2 ⅝"; Late 19th C.
Bottom: poplar cloth, silk, and kid leather.
3¼" x 2½"; Late 19th C.
Enfield Shaker Village, NH
Enfield Shaker Museum, NH

Sewing Bag
Poplar cloth, silk, and kid leather.
7¼" x 2¼"; Late 19th C.
Enfield Shaker Village, NH
Enfield Shaker Museum, NH

Alfred, ME

Catalog
Black ink on white paper.
Alfred Shaker Village, ME
7¾" x 5½"; 1908.
Private Collection

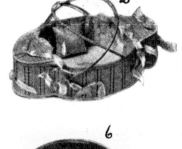

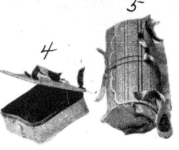

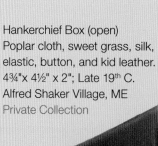

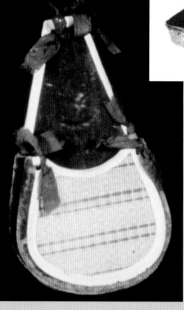

Pocket Watch Holder
Poplar cloth, velvet, silk,
and kid leather.
5¼" x 3¼" x 1'; Late 19th C.
Alfred Shaker Village, ME
Private Collection

Hankerchief Box (open)
Poplar cloth, sweet grass, silk,
elastic, button, and kid leather.
4¾"x 4½" x 2"; Late 19th C.
Alfred Shaker Village, ME
Private Collection

Jewelry Case (closed)
Poplar cloth, silk, and kid leather.
4½" x 4" x 1½"; Late 19th C.
Alfred Shaker Village, ME
Private Collection

Work Casket (closed)
Poplar cloth, silk, velvet, and kid leather.
5¾" x 3½" x 3"; Late 19th C.
Alfred Shaker Village, ME
Private Collection

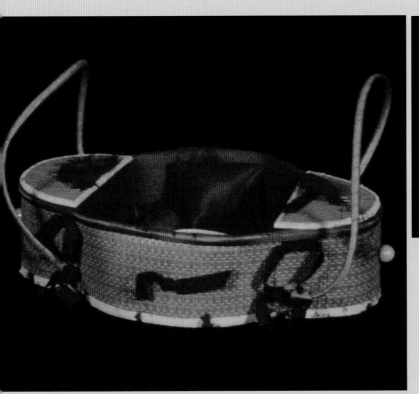

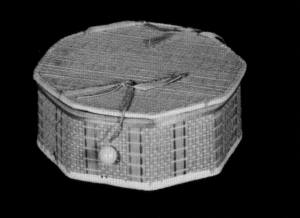

Small Octagon (closed)
Poplar cloth, silk, elastic, button, and kid leather.
4⅛" x 4⅛" x 1⅝"; Late 19th C.
Alfred Shaker Village, ME
Private Collection

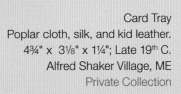

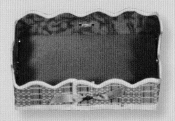

Bifold
Poplar cloth, poplar wrapped handle, silk, pin cushion,
emery, and kid leather,
7½" x 5½" x 2"; Late 19th C.
Alfred Shaker Village, ME
Private Collection

Card Tray
Poplar cloth, silk, and kid leather.
4¾" x 3⅛" x 1¼"; Late 19th C.
Alfred Shaker Village, ME
Private Collection

Catalog (pages 6 and 7)
Black ink on white paper.
7¾" x 5½"; 1910.
Sabbathday Lake Shaker Village, ME
Private Collection

The articles in PLATE I are Poplar Goods, satin lined, excepting Nos. 2 and 7, which are lined in velvet.

Bottom measurements and prices follow.

No. 1, Stud Box. Two sizes, 2¼ inches square, 30c; 3¼ inches square, 45c

No. 2, Gents' Jewelry Case. 4¼ in. x 3 in., 75c

No. 3, Glove Case. 12¼ in. x 3⅝ in., $1.50

No. 4, Necktie Case. Two sizes, 15¼ in. x 2⅝ in., $1.40; 15¼ in. x 3¼ in., $1.60

No. 6, Silk Box. Two sizes, 4 in. x 2 in., 45c; 6¼ in. x 2¼ in., 50c

No. 7, Ladies' Jewelry Case. Three Sizes, 7¼ in. x 4¼ in., $1.25; 8 in. x 5¼ in., $1.50; 8½ in. x 5¼ in., $1.75

No. 8, Handkerchief Box. Two sizes, 5 inches square, 90c; 6 in. square, $1.10

No. 9, Card Case. 8¼ in. x 4⅜ in., $1.00

Square Basket Cushion
Poplar cloth, velvet, and kid leather.
2" x 2" x 1½"; Late 19th C.
Sabbathday Lake Shaker Village, ME
Private Collection

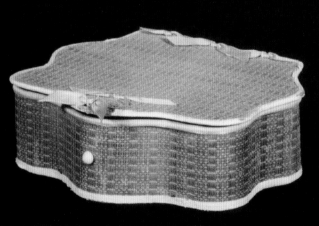

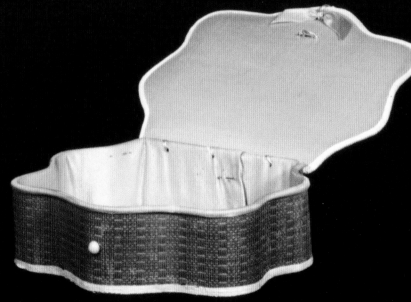

Sewing Box, (closed and open)
Poplar cloth, silk, button, and kid leather.
8½" x 7½" x 2½"; Late 19th C.
Sabbathday Lake Shaker Village, ME
Private Collection

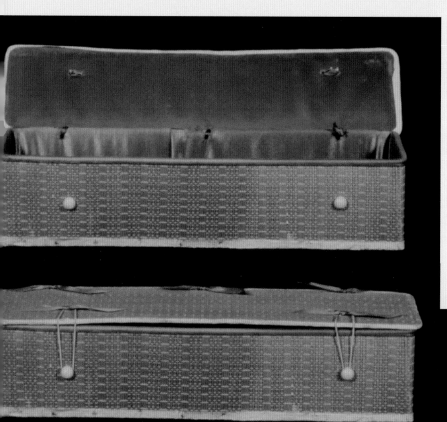

Glove Case (open and closed)
Poplar cloth, silk, elastic, buttons, and kid leather.
12¼" x 3⅝" x 3"; Late 19th C.
Sabbathday Lake Shaker Village, ME
Private Collection

Gent's Jewelry Case
Poplar cloth, velvet, button, and kid leather.
4¾" x 3" x 1½"; Late 19th C.
Sabbathday Lake Shaker Village, ME
Private Collection

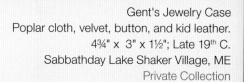

Small Work Box
Poplar cloth, silk, elastic, button, and kid leather.
4¼" x 3" x 2"; Late 19th C.
Sabbathday Lake Shaker Village, ME
Private Collection

Stud Box
Poplar cloth, silk, elastic, button, and kid leather.
3¼" x 3¼" x 2"; Late 19th C.
Sabbathday Lake Shaker Village, ME
Private Collection

Sabbathday Lake, ME

Gents' Jewelry Case
Poplar cloth, velvet, button, elastic, and kid leather.
4½" x 3½" x 1¼"; 1900
Sabbathday Lake Shaker Village, ME
Western Reserve Historical Society, OH

Ladies' Jewelry Cases
Poplar cloth, velvet, silk, elastic, button, and
kid leather.
8¾" x 6" x 1¾"; 1900.
Sabbathday Lake Shaker Village, ME
Western Reserve Historical Society, OH

All articles in PLATE II are Work Boxes made of poplar, satin lined. Nos. 12, 13, 14 and 16 have full furnishings, namely: pincushion, needle book, emery and wax. No. 15 has emery and wax with needle book on cover. No. 11 has emery and wax.

Bottom measurements and prices follow.

No. 11, Small Octagon. 4 inches, 65c

No. 12, Hexagon. 4⅜ inches, $1.00

No. 13, Octagon. Two sizes, 5¼ inches, $1.50; 6¼ inches, $2.00

No. 14, Open Work Box. Three sizes, 6 in. x 3⅜ in. $1.00; 6⅜ in. x 4⅜ in. $1.20 and 7¼ in. x 4¼ in., $1.40

No. 15, Small Work Box. 4¼ in. x 3 in., 75c

No. 16, Square Work Box. Three sizes, 4⅜ inches, $1.25; 5¼ inches, $1.50; 6¼ inches, $2.00

Catalog (page 9)
Black ink on white paper.
7¾" x 5½"; 1910.
Sabbathday Lake Shaker Village, ME
Private Collection

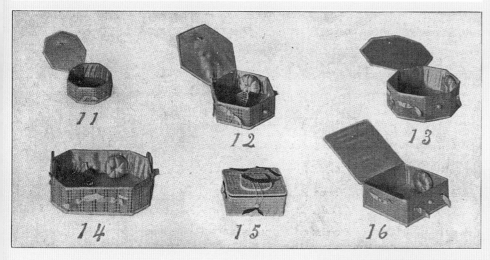

Catalog (page 10)
Black ink on white paper.
7¾" x 5½"; 1910.
Sabbathday Lake Shaker Village, ME
Private Collection

Hexagon (closed and open)
Poplar cloth, silk, elastic, button, and kid leather.
4⅜" x 4⅜" x 2¼"; Late 19th C.
Sabbathday Lake Shaker Village, ME
Private Collection

Sabbathday Lake, ME

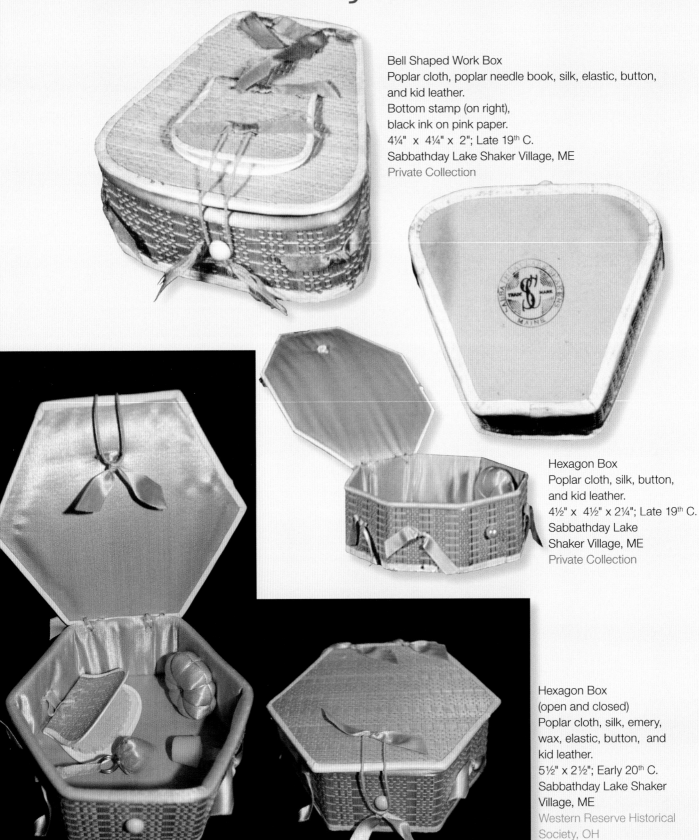

Bell Shaped Work Box
Poplar cloth, poplar needle book, silk, elastic, button,
and kid leather.
Bottom stamp (on right),
black ink on pink paper.
4¼" x 4¼" x 2"; Late 19th C.
Sabbathday Lake Shaker Village, ME
Private Collection

Hexagon Box
Poplar cloth, silk, button,
and kid leather.
4½" x 4½" x 2¼"; Late 19th C.
Sabbathday Lake
Shaker Village, ME
Private Collection

Hexagon Box
(open and closed)
Poplar cloth, silk, emery,
wax, elastic, button, and
kid leather.
5½" x 2½"; Early 20th C.
Sabbathday Lake Shaker
Village, ME
Western Reserve Historical
Society, OH

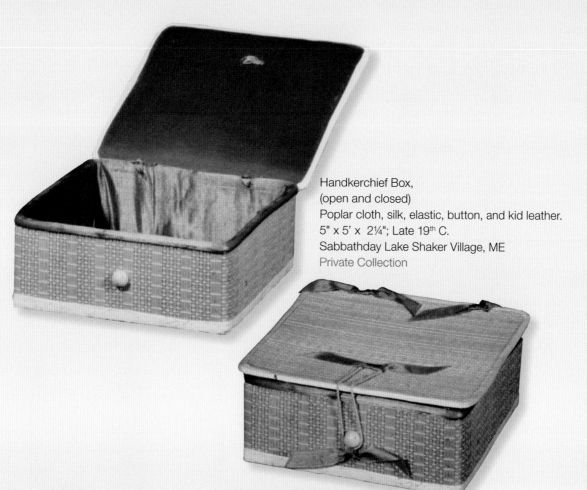

Handkerchief Box,
(open and closed)
Poplar cloth, silk, elastic, button, and kid leather.
5" x 5' x 2¼"; Late 19th C.
Sabbathday Lake Shaker Village, ME
Private Collection

CONCERT ON POLAND SPRING HOUSE PIAZZA

Photo
Woman with a poplarware sewing box on her lap.
Photo taken from the *Hilltop* Newspaper.
Poland Springs Hotel, Poland Springs, ME, July, 1918.
The Poland Spring Preservation Society, Poland Springs, ME

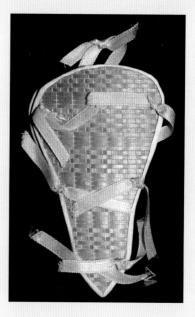

Scissor Case/Sheath
Poplar cloth, silk, and kid leather.
3¼" x 2"; 1900.
Probably Sabbathday Lake Shaker Village, ME
Western Reserve Historical Society, OH

Canterbury, NH

Poplar Boxes
Poplar cloth, silk, emery, wax,
elastic, button, and kid leather.
Octagons: 7¼" x 5" x 2¾",
Square Box: 5" x 5" x 2¾";
First Quarter 20th C.
Canterbury Shaker Village, NH
Enfield Shaker Village, NH

Poplar Box Bottom
Wallpaper trimmed in kid leather;
Mid 20th C.
Canterbury Shaker Village, NH
Enfield Shaker Village, NH

Poplar Box
Poplar cloth, cotton, silk, elastic, button,
and kid leather.
4¼" x 3" x 1⅝"; 1950.
Canterbury Shaker Village, NH
Shaker Museum | Mount Lebanon, NY

Poplar Box (closed and open)
Poplar cloth, cotton, elastic, button,
and kid leather.
4½" x 3" x 1⅝"; 1953.
Canterbury Shaker Village, NH
Shaker Museum | Mount Lebanon, NY

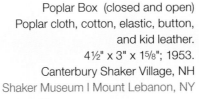

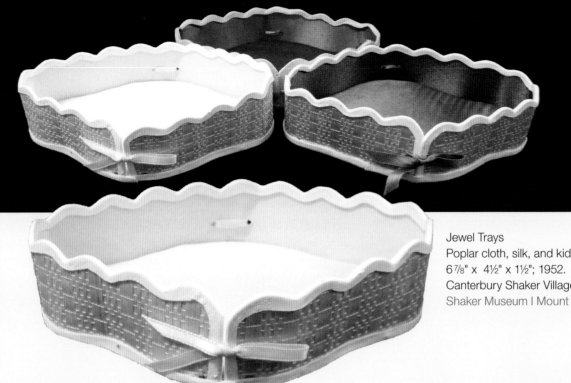

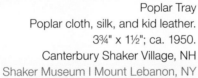

Jewel Trays
Poplar cloth, silk, and kid leather.
6⅞" x 4½" x 1½"; 1952.
Canterbury Shaker Village, NH
Shaker Museum I Mount Lebanon, NY

Poplar Tray
Poplar cloth, silk, and kid leather.
3¾" x 1½"; ca. 1950.
Canterbury Shaker Village, NH
Shaker Museum I Mount Lebanon, NY

Handkerchief Box (open and closed)
Poplar cloth, silk, elastic, button, and kid leather.
5" x 2¾"; Mid. 20th C.
Canterbury Shaker Village, ME
Hancock Shaker Village, MA

Silk-top Basket or Button Basket (two views)
Black ash and silk. Round quadrifoil bottom
with wide crossed bands at center.
3½" diam., 1" visible base, 2½" silk
drawstring top; Mid-late 19ᵗʰ C.
Mount Lebanon Shaker Village, NY
New York State Museum, NY

SHAKER FANCY BASKETS

with Nathan Taylor

*"'Here are pretty little baskets, filled with love,'" they sang in meeting,
"'and I've brought them to you on my silver wings, says mother's little dove.'"*[1]

T HE STORY OF SHAKER BASKETS falls neatly into two categories, utilitarian and fancy, a useful division that began with the leadership of Elder Brother John Farrington, (1760–1833). One of the earliest converts to Shaker belief, Farrington was a basket maker and under his direction the New Lebanon Shaker Brethren made utility baskets for the Community, for use in fields, gardens, orchards, shops, and dwellings. During Farrington's tenure, the Brethren borrowed from vernacular styles to make these early baskets, modeling their large utilitarian pieces on those they bought from nearby Native Americans and itinerant basket makers.[2] Each was made from start to finish by a single Brother and so the baskets lacked the uniformity that later made them so sought after and recognizable. Variations in a basket's weight, height, and handle style depended on its designated purpose, as well as on the distinctive features of an individual craftsman's workmanship.

The preferred Shaker basket material was black ash, *fraxinus nigra*, these ash uprights or staves started out as the base and rose vertically to form the walls; the sides were built with horizontal black ash weavers that interwove and connected the vertical uprights to make its body. The basket's top was further leveled with a single binder row that is woven back on top of itself. This was the final leveling row. Each Stave was pointed and folded over the binder row and tucked into the weaver row below it to seal the body into one unit.[3] A pair of rims inside and out covered and reinforced the top row and made up its skeleton, and handles were notched to hold them in place on the rim. The two rims with the handle were then lashed around the binder to the body to complete the basket. The body and the skeleton became one, giving the basket its strength and rigidity.[4]

A decade prior to the 1830s, Daniel Boler (1804–1892), under the tutelage of Elder Farrington, decided to make an industry of fancy basket making. Another young Shaker apprentice by the name of Daniel Crosman (1810–1885) rigged up much of the new power machinery to facilitate basket making.[5] And so the Shakers, having already provided them-

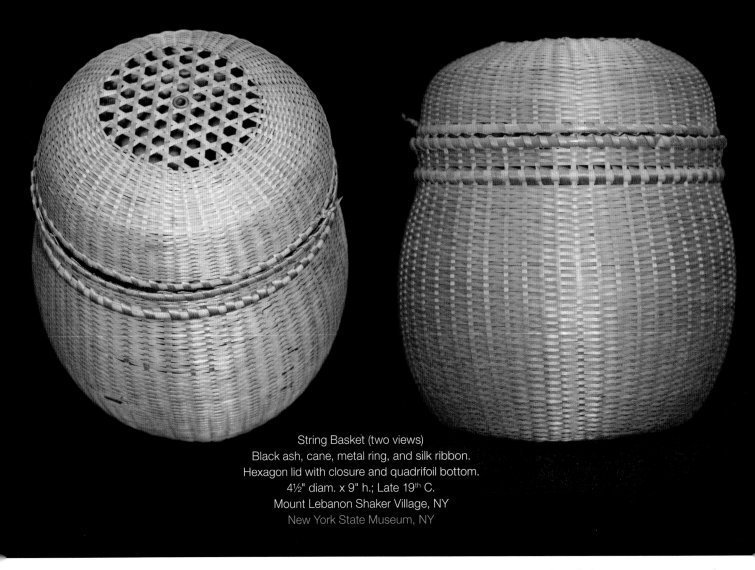

String Basket (two views)
Black ash, cane, metal ring, and silk ribbon.
Hexagon lid with closure and quadrifoil bottom.
4½" diam. x 9" h.; Late 19ᵗʰ C.
Mount Lebanon Shaker Village, NY
New York State Museum, NY

selves with an abundance of utility baskets, decided to turn much of their attention and well-developed expertise and tooling practices to the production of lighter, more finely woven baskets. They called this new line of products "fancy baskets."

From the 1830s to 1892, fancy baskets were designed and made by the Shaker Sisters for a variety of domestic and commercial purposes and were much in demand in the World beyond their Communities. Smaller, lighter and more refined than working baskets, Sister's fancy baskets generated a lucrative stream of income that helped support their Community through the combined economic challenges posed by the Industrial Revolution on one hand and the dwindling male population in the Shaker Communities on the other.[6]

Both the process of creation, which entailed developing a product and managing its production, and the methods of their final sale were efforts that remained entirely in the hands of the Sisters. A core group of five young Sisters led the industry until its end: Sister Julia Ann Scott (1839–1918), Sister Elizabeth Cantrell (1832–1906), Sister Ann Maria Graves (1833–1914), Sister Augusta Stone (1836–1908), and Sister Cornelia French (1840–1917).[7]

A fancy basket is made up of the same structural elements as a utility basket. It was made of ash splint of a smaller size. Unlike a utility basket that was made for a more rugged outdoor use, many fancy baskets were made for indoor delicate use.

Fancy baskets were not only made by women, they were made for women. Fancy baskets were specifically designed and made to appeal to the broader market in what the Shakers called "the World." Fancy at the time implied superior grade, extra fine, intricately made, suitable for select patronage—exactly the kind of wealthy and sophisticated buyers who made the baskets such a profitable enterprise.

STYLES

THE SHAKERS brought to their work that sense of perfection and order emblematic of the ideals that infused their way of life. Their fancy baskets were woven in a Shaker Victorian style[8] suitable for knitting or sewing implements, fruit, eggs, and herbs.[9] The Sisters, in addition to designing a wide variety of shapes for a wide variety of uses, also undertook the labor-intensive work of fabricating the baskets, and often finished the work by outfitting the interiors. Many fancy baskets were made for sewing. They held accoutrements such as a pin cushion, emery, needle book and thread wax, all made by the Sisters.[10] *The Memorandum of Baskets, etc., Kept by the Basketmaker* lists twenty styles in varying sizes, whose designs remained consistent from 1855 to 1875. *The Memorandum* includes descriptions of each style and directions for the number of uprights, the width of weavers, the rim length, and the lashing style around the rim.[11]

Among the most popular Shaker baskets listed in *The Memorandum* is the "knife" basket, all with a rectangular bottom, and sides that are either perpendicular or rise with a slight flare from the base.

Knife Basket
Weaver ratio, 4:1
6¾" l. x 3¼" w. x 2½" h.; 1860–1880
Mount Lebanon shaker Village, NY
Western Reserve Historical Society, OH

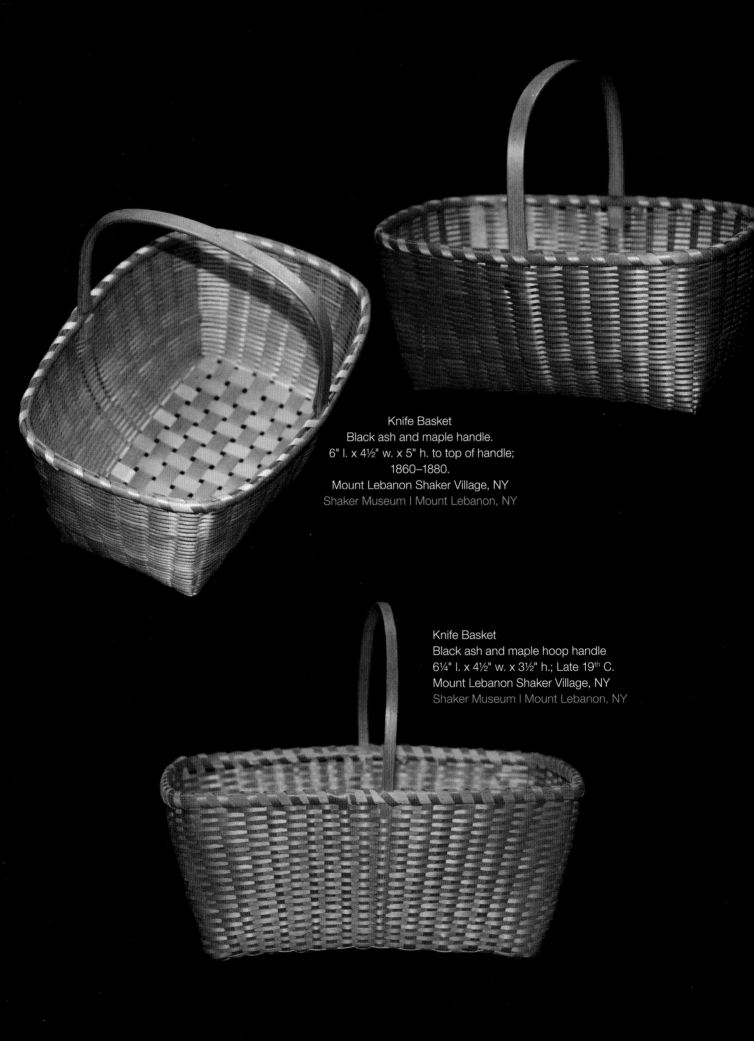

Knife Basket
Black ash and maple handle.
6" l. x 4½" w. x 5" h. to top of handle;
1860–1880.
Mount Lebanon Shaker Village, NY
Shaker Museum I Mount Lebanon, NY

Knife Basket
Black ash and maple hoop handle
6¼" l. x 4½" w. x 3½" h.; Late 19th C.
Mount Lebanon Shaker Village, NY
Shaker Museum I Mount Lebanon, NY

The knife basket got its name from its straight sides and square bottom corners, as tight and crisp as if they had been cut with a knife.[12] It would have a center bonnet handle across the basket. A smaller one would have ear handles on each end, or a long handle end to end like a carpenter's tool box. This basket was among the most varied and most popular.[13] Other fancy baskets included in the Memorandum are the square bottom, round-top "fruit baskets," one of the first the Shakers made for sale; the "cat head" basket, similar to the fruit basket only smaller and lighter; and the "kitten head" basket, a diminutive version of the "cat." The feline association comes from the peaked corners of the bases that resemble a cat's ears. Kitten head baskets are identifiable by turning a finished basked upside down and looking at the shape of a kitten's head in the basket. This is accomplished by making the center of the base rise and the corners to drop as it is woven, an effect that was often achieved through the use of wooden molds that helped guide the weaver's efforts. The three larger sizes of cat head baskets follow a simple progression from the three smaller versions of kitten heads.[14]

Kitten Head Basket
Black ash and maple bonnet handle.
3½" diam. x 2½" h.; 1860–1880.
Mount Lebanon Shaker Village, NY
Shaker Museum I Mount Lebanon, NY

Cat Head Basket
Black ash and maple handle.
4" diam. x 3⅛" h.; Mid. 19th C.
Mount Lebanon Shaker Village, NY
Shaker Museum I Mount Lebanon, NY

Quadrifoil Tub (two views)
Black ash, quadrifoil base.
6¾" diam. x 2" h.; 1860–1880.
Mount Lebanon Shaker Village, NY
Shaker Museum I Mount Lebanon, NY

A very popular style was a tub. It got its name from its perfectly sharp upturned sides resembling those of a tin washtub. Unique to Mount Lebanon, these round baskets had a "quadrifoil" [*sic*] twilled base resembling a four-leaf clover and ear handles. The basket came in four sizes.[15] Hexagon baskets were another popular type. This basket was a hexagonal open work basket, most often lidded. Many examples started out with a hexagonal base and wove to a round top.[16] The baskets were generally intended for use as a sewing kit.

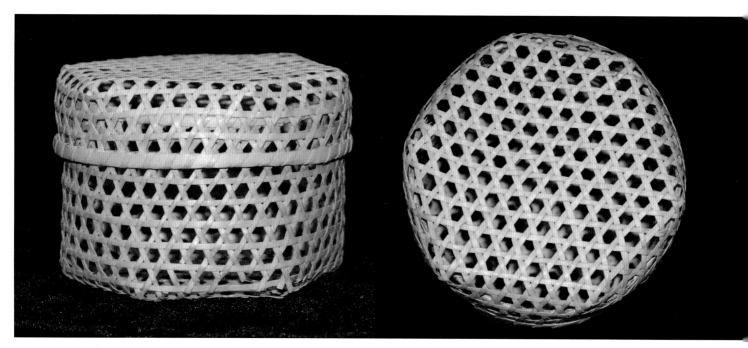

Covered Hexagonal Basket and Lid. Black ash; 3¾" diam. x 2¼" h.; 1860–1885. Mount Lebanon Shaker Village, NY
Shaker Museum I Mount Lebanon, NY

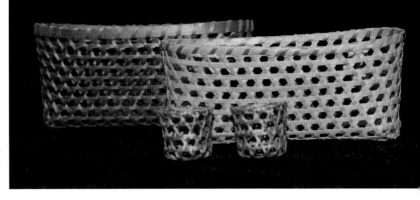

Hexagonal Weave Baskets
L-Black ash, R- Palm leaf with black ash lashing
Front- Black ash, thimble holders.
Thimble holders were made by Native Americans.
Shakers used their own in furnishing sewing baskets.
Left; 4" l. x 2" w. x 2" h.; Right; 4" l. x 1¾" w. x 1¾" h;
Front; ⅞" diam. x ¾" h.; Late 19th C.
Mount Lebanon Shaker Village, NY
Shaker Museum I Mount Lebanon, NY

Sawtooth Basket. Black ash;
2¼" l. x 1¾" w. x 1¼" h.; 1860–1880
Mount Lebanon Shaker Village, NY
Shaker Museum I Mount Lebanon, NY

Furnished baskets were outfitted by the Sisters in the Second Order with a pin cushion, emery, wax cake, and a needle book usually made from woven poplar with felt leaves.[17]

PRODUCTION AND SALES

At New Lebanon, two generations of Ministry Elders were committed utility basket makers, ensuring that the Community supported the industry and that the baskets measured up to the highest standards.[18] This allowed for the continuation of the basket-making tradition to be carried on by the Sisters; however, it was fancy-basket production that took center stage. Basketry occupied the Shakers from autumn to spring. Fifty-one women were involved at one time or another between the 1830s and 1890s, with a core of five who dedicated themselves to the industry for the twenty-five years of peak production—from 1850 to 1875. Augmented by a rotating group of ten to fourteen others, these five Sisters produced 71,244 baskets.[19] A journal entry from 1872 records: "Sale Work by the Sisters in the First Order, Splint baskets of various kinds 1754."[20]

Two years later, the record continues: "Sister's Sale Work, Splint baskets made 1,407."[21]

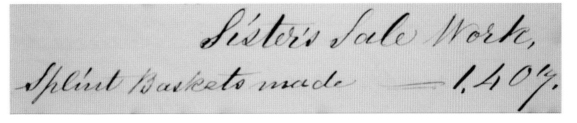

The Mount Lebanon Sisters managed sales and shipping, at first limited to the "Office Store" in the Trustees' building and local outlets.[22] Soon, the Church Family Sisters launched into both wholesale and retail marketing. They made excursions to neighboring communities, soliciting and delivering orders, and shipped baskets regularly to New York City, Albany, and Philadelphia. Wholesale selling extended across the country and as far afield as England.[23]

FINAL DAYS

In 1875, a fire destroyed eight buildings at Mount Lebanon, as well as baskets, tools, molds, machinery, and raw materials. Sister Anna Dodgson reported the losses: "Fancy Work 1875 lost in fire 350 splint basket[s] and 100 poplar work."[24] That year the First Order recorded production of "Splint baskets 188." A year later, in 1876, production had rebounded: "Splint baskets 834" and seemed to be on the way to a full recovery.[25] Anna Dodgson's journal reports 350 splint baskets in 1878, with sale work done by Sisters. In the following years, her journal records:

> **1881** Splint baskets small 200, splint baskets twilled 150.
> **1882** 41 round covered twilled baskets, 200 small twilled baskets, 60 large twilled, 30 heart.
> **1883** Baskets splint many covered 160, kitten baskets for silk tops 137, ovals for silk tops 22.[26]

Production sputtered soon after this, however, and never resumed its former volume. With Elder Daniel Boler's death in 1892, the industry continued to decline, a temporary resurgence in 1897 notwithstanding. "An effort is being made," a Sister wrote, "to start up the basket industry left by Boler."[27] By this time, though, the Shakers' use of black ash had substantially depleted their supply. They sought ash as far as forty miles away, but often what they found proved unsatisfactory.[28] The lack of raw materials, coupled with the deeply felt loss of Elder Boler, brought the fancy-basket-making industry to a close, although a few baskets were still made over the next half century.[29]

FANCY BRUSHES AND DUSTERS

Hat Brushes
Horse hair, velvet, silk, cherry and walnut wood.
8½" to 10"; Early 20th C.
Sabbathday Lake Shaker Village, ME or
Alfred Shaker Village, ME
Photo by Kent Ruesswick
Canterbury Brush Works, Canterbury, NH

10
FANCY BRUSHES
AND DUSTERS

*I must hasten for I hope to make between six and seven
hundred brushes this spring. This summer will come and
the sales, as usual, we must work if we expect to live another
winter. The same. Year after year.*

—Journal of Sister Aurelia Mace, Sabbathday Lake, Maine[1]

A FINE SENSE OF order and cleanliness remained crucial to the Shaker way of life, virtues instilled by the founder of their sect, Mother Ann Lee. "Clean your room well," Mother Ann wrote, "for good spirits will not live where there is dirt. There is no dirt in heaven."[2] Many of the spare furnishings of Shaker design, from desks and built-in cupboards to sewing boxes and their accompanying accoutrements, reflect this ideal of keeping things uncluttered and in their place (if not out of sight), as well as dust- and dirt-free. Shaker hat brushes offered yet another example of that combination of practicality and ingenuity that characterized, in this case, all that the Sisters made for sale.

Sister Aurelia Mace (1835–1910) is credited with revitalizing the horsehair brush industry at Sabbathday Lake in the last quarter of the nineteenth century, to add to the Shaker Sisters' fancy goods repertoire in support of their Community. Canterbury also made and sold fancy brushes at around the same time. At the Sabbathday Lake Community in Maine, hat brushes, made in two sizes, sold for thirty and fifty cents each at the beginning of the twentieth century. According to the Consumer Price Index, these brushes would sell for around $8.00 and $13.00 in 2019. "The hat brush works very nicely on velvet of all kinds," notes the Sabbathday Lake *Catalog of Fancy Goods* from 1910.

Sister Mace's idea proved inspirational and timely. All felted hats, no matter what the shape, needed an instrument for cleaning them and horsehair brushes were ideal for the task. In the world of fashion, men's hats—top hats, bowlers, derbies, fedoras—were on the rise as an elegant accessory and as evidence of social standing and profession, peaking in popularity at the turn of the twentieth century. Women's hats, too, whose styles evolved with the times, remained essential daily and evening wear.

Construction of the brushes was a labor-intensive process. They were made from 3¾-inch-wide strips of horsehair cloth, sewn together to make up an 83-inch length.[3] The Sisters, or more often young girls (who had not yet signed the Shaker Covenant, committing them to the Shaker way of life), were given this onerous task, referred to in their journals as "raveling." This meant removing the warp from the cloth to expose a length of horsetail hair, approximately 2¾-inches long, leaving a one-inch intact strip of cloth running the entire length. This strip was then wrapped around the brush handle, glued and

Horse Hair Cloth
Raveled horse hair cloth.
3¾" w; Early 20th C.
Canterbury Shaker Village, NH
Canterbury Brush Works, Canterbury, NH

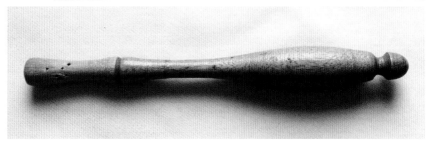

Brush Handle
Cherry wood.
6⅜"; Early 20th C.
Canterbury Shaker Village, NH
Canterbury Brush Works, Canterbury, NH

nailed in place, with the topmost part of the wrap tucked under and glued for a smooth, secure finish.[4] Handles were turned by Brothers and were made from maple or cherry woods. A velvet cover was added to conceal the portion of the horsehair cloth surrounding the handle, pulled tight, and sewn down the side, hiding the cloth and nails.[5] Silk ribbons were usually tied at the top of the handle and above the skirt.

Fancy brushes produced at Canterbury, New Hampshire, and Sabbathday Lake, Maine, were similar except for the skirt edges and handle shape. The Canterbury Shakers made their brush handles more bulbous and their velvet skirts were cut straight across or tucked under to provide a simple hem. At Sabbathday Lake the velvet skirts have pinked edging (cut with pinking shears) and the handles were thinner.[6]

Hat Brush
Horse hair, velvet, and cherry wood.
8⅜"; Early 20th C.
Sabbathday Lake Village, ME
Canterbury Brush Works, Canterbury, NH

The Sabbathday Lake Church Family Record allows us to peek behind the scenes:

> **[1890]**
> **Wed. Mar. 24** *Sister at the office commence to wind their brushes.*
> **Wed. July 9** *Ada [Cummings] and Aurelia go to the [Poland] Springs. Meet with good success. Sell 9 hair brushes.*
> **Tues. Aug. 5** *Aurelia went to Lewiston to get material for her hair brushes. Pliny and Clara Blanchard go with her.*
>
> **[1894]**
> **Thurs. April 5** *The little girls are raveling horsehair cloth for Aurelia to make into brushes for sale.*
> **Thurs. May 4** *Sisters are making horsehair brushes.*
>
> **[1896]**
> **Wed. Mar. 24** *Sister at the office commence to wind their brushes.*
>
> **[1897]**
> **Fri. Feb. 26** *Little girls raveling hair cloth for the office sisters.*[7]

Elder Otis Sawyer, of Sabbathday Lake, documented a successful day of fancy goods sales on July 25, 1898: ". . . sold a lot of carriers, dolls, brushes, needle books."[8] In 1901, also at Sabbathday Lake, the Church Journal notes that on "Tues. April 2 Children are raveling hair-cloth," followed by this entry: "Wed May 29 Aurelia Has [*sic*] put on the handles [to] almost 700 hair brushes – that job is finished today. They now await the velvet [skirt] and [silk] ribbon."[9]

Hat Brushes
Horse hair, velvet, maple, cherry,
and walnut wood
8½" to 10"; Early 20th C.
1 & 2 Canterbury Shaker Village, NH
3 & 4 Sabbathday Lake Shaker Village, ME
or Alfred Shaker Village, ME
Photo by Kent Ruesswick
Canterbury Brush Works, Canterbury, NH

WOOL DUSTER, 40c.

11

Catalog
Products of Intelligence and Diligence
Black ink on off-white paper.
7" x 4 5/8"; 1908, p.11.
Mount Lebanon Shaker Village, NY
Private Collection

Duster
Dyed wool and maple wood.
10½"; Early 20th C.
Mount Lebanon Shaker village, NY
Enfield Shaker Museum, NH

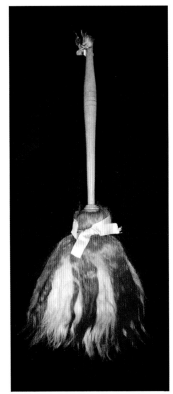

Dusters
Dyed wool and maple wood.
15½"; Early 20th C.
Mount Lebanon Shaker
Village, NY
Shaker Museum | Mount
Lebanon, NY

Duster
Dyed wool and maple wood.
9½"; Early 29th C.
Mount Lebanon Shaker
Village, NY
Shaker Heritage Society, NY

Cardigan Sweater
White wool and mother-of-pearl.
28" x 16"; First Quarter 20th C.
Canterbury Shaker Village, NH
Canterbury Shaker Village, NH

A BRIEF HISTORY OF THE SWEATER

THE FIRST SWEATERS as we know them originated on the Channel Islands of Guernsey and Jersey, knit by fishermen and sailors' wives from wool whose natural oils protected the men against dampness and cold. The use of the "jersey," so called, spread throughout Europe, particularly among workingmen. In the 1880s, these woolen "vests" or "jerseys" were worn by rowers, and called sweaters—the word dates from 1828—meaning "clothing worn to produce sweating and reduce weight." By the 1920s, French designers Coco Chanel and Jeanne Lanvin had introduced sweaters into their haute couture collections.[1] The sweater's newfound place in fashion was noted at the time in the New York periodical, *The Haberdasher:*

> All of us can remember when the sweater was merely synonymous with an
> overheated perspiring athlete. . . Humble of origin, like many other things
> it has lived down its reputation as merely utilitarian, and has assumed its
> rightful place in men's apparel as a thing of beauty and adornment.
> Its predictability still remains an assured fact.[2]

1. https://www.britanica.com / topic/ sweater (Accessed 9/15/18)
2. Arthur Beaumont, "Prophesying a Profit in Sweaters," published in *The Haberdasher*, November, 1922, 59.

Auto Collar Sweater
Red wool and mother-of-pearl.
28" x 20"; First Quarter 20th C.
Canterbury Shaker Village, NH
Canterbury Shaker Village, NH

11
SHAKER SWEATERS

Shaker Sweater – Heavyweight rib-knit fabric
developed by members of the Shaker sect.

1900 Nov. 1. *The rush for sweaters not yet abated*
although most of October was spent by the sisters
filling orders.[1]

THE SHAKER SISTERS had always knit sweaters, stockings, undergarments, mittens, and hats for themselves and for sale to the public. But when an opportunity to fill a large order of sweaters for the public came along, in what now seems a turning point in the history of the Shaker fancy goods industry, the shift to knitting by machine, already in use in many Shaker Villages, proved providential.[2] That first order, the one that led to the establisment of the sweater making industry, came in 1886 when, according to the archives at Canterbury Shaker Community, a man from England "brought a sweater to us and asked if we could make one like it."

"We had no machine for that purpose, but in April 1886, Mr. S.W. Kent came to us with a very large order of sweaters, [asking] if we could fill it."[3] From then on, the Shaker Sisters "knit [sweaters] by motor" to meet the demand, as Canterbury Sister Josephine Wilson (1866–1946) observed in her diary nearly thirty years later.[4] Using an Aiken knitting machine borrowed from the Shaker Society at Enfield, New Hampshire, the Sisters fulfilled the request and "before December 25, had shipped an order of 60 dozen sweaters to New York. This was the beginning of a most profitable trade."[5]

So began the Shakers' more than forty-year commitment to making sweaters in large quantities, and their corresponding investment in knitting machines that grew increasingly sophisticated over the years. Knitting had been an important activity for the Shaker Sisters in the second half of the nineteenth century, mainly in the wintertime. Sweater sales went on to create a substantial, profitable, coordinated industry.[6]

Occasionally, business came to the Canterbury Shaker's doorstep, as in the example cited above. The Sisters there also sought it out. In a Canterbury Journal entry for February, 1894, for example, it reads: "Emeline Hart, and E.J. Aiken go to North Adams [Massachusetts] to drum up trade on sweaters."[7]

To keep pace with the newfound demand for these garments, the Shakers frequently upgraded their knitting machines, first developed in England in the late eighteenth century, to take advantage of the latest technology. The Sisters soon replaced their J.B. Aiken's flatbed knitting machine, which knit single web only, with the Lamb machine that knit double webbing for both sleeves and body, and could be adapted for different grades of yarn. This machine, developed in 1863 by the Reverend Isaac Lamb (1840–1906), a Baptist clergyman from Michigan, was the first successful flat (as opposed to circular) knitting machine to be designed in the United States.[8] Revolutionary at the time, Lamb machine that the Shakers purchased in 1887 for $195 from the Lamb Knitting Co., in Chicopee, Massachusetts, used two rows of latch needles on an angle to each other.[9] The Lamb could be operated at a rate of 4,000 knots a minute, was capable of a variety of stitches, and knit both tubular (without a seam), or flat in a ribbed or plain (stockinette) stitch.[10] Its adjustable width made it adaptable for a variety of Shaker products in addition to sweaters, including stocking legs and cardigan jackets.[11] Altogether, the Canterbury Shakers purchased five knitting machines between 1887 and 1903, ranging in price from $195 to $904.[12]

Frequent references to the acquisition of knitting machines and to their foibles appear in the Canterbury journals alongside entries about promotional expeditions, details of sweater production, and brief notes on sales trips and shipments. By this time, the Shaker sweater, along with the Dorothy cloak and Poplarware, dominated production and sales of the fancy good items that drew a worldly clientele to Canterbury's own gift store and to displays at resort hotels.[13] On May 13, 1890, for example: "E.A. Stratton and L.A. Shephard leave home for New York to consult a party in regard to buying sweaters made in Canterbury." Their errand appears to have been successful, for two days later, on May 15: "E.A. Stratton and L.A. Shephard return from New York with an order for 100 doz. sweaters." Something must have gone awry with the knitting machines, however, for in mid-July of that year, we read: "Br. John Cummings goes to Concord to have work [done] on knitting machine." [14]

The journal from 1891, reveals a similar pattern of prolific output, alongside investment in machinery to support their new industry:

> **Oct. 31** *The giant sweater knitter arrived today. This machine was made to order by Sandborn of Chicopee Falls. . . cost $900, weight 700 pounds.* **Nov. 3** *S. Bartlett the Concord machinist comes to adjust the Giant Knitter.* **Nov. 11** *Knitter in successful operation today.* **Nov. 16** *An order of 7 doz. sweaters to be forwarded immediately.* **Nov. 28** *Sixty doz. Sweaters have been shipped for New York since Oct. 1st.*[15]

Subsequent years saw the Sisters investing in several new knitters, with occasional mechanical problems interrupting the steady flow of work.

> **1905** *Sisters J.H. Fish and H.A. Wilson leave home Sept. 10 to order new Lamb Knitter of the Co. at Chicopee Falls.*[16]
>
> **1907** *A new Circular Web No. 2 Lamb Knitting Machine was ordered Sept. 11 1906 of the Lamb Knitting Machine Co., Chicopee Falls, Mass. The machine arrived early in Jan. of this year, but when adjusted by Mr. Eaton, engineer of the Co., who called Jan. 16 – 19, it proved unsatisfactory and was shipped back to the firm. A second machine to be made according to the text of order was insisted up.*[17]
>
> **1908** *The new Lamb Knitting Machine arrived Mar. 5 and was installed to take [the] place of the old Aiken now past usefulness. It proved itself satisfactory in every way.*[18]

The success of the sweaters depended in large part on the use of only high-quality materials, as it did with other Shaker products. The Sisters purchased two-ply (two strands twisted together) yarn in four weights—medium light, medium, heavy, and extra heavy—spun from pure Australian wool and produced exclusively for the Canterbury Shakers by S. B. and B.W. Fleisher of Philadelphia.[19]

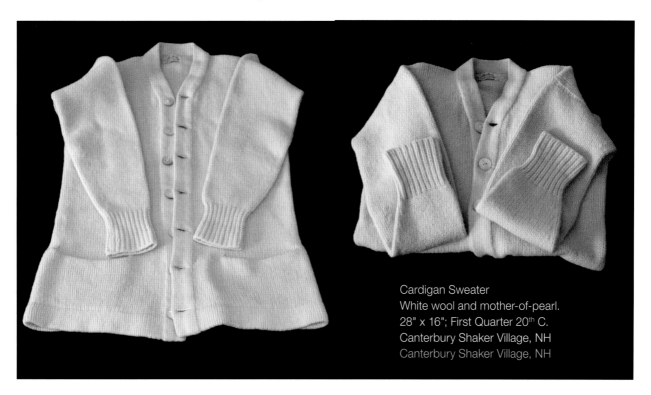

Cardigan Sweater
White wool and mother-of-pearl.
28" x 16"; First Quarter 20th C.
Canterbury Shaker Village, NH
Canterbury Shaker Village, NH

Pullover Sweater
Navy blue and light gray wool.
25" x 18¾"; 1930.
Machine knit by Edith Clark for Alberta Kirkpatrick (Husen).
Canterbury Shaker Village, NH
Canterbury Shaker Village, NH

Shaker Sweater Pieces
Arm pieces.
Canterbury Shaker Village, NH
Canterbury Shaker Village, NH

Cardigan Sweater
Black wool and mother-of-pearl.
31½" x 18¾"; First Quarter 20th C.
Canterbury Shaker Village, NH
Canterbury Shaker Village, NH

Most Shaker sweaters came in two distinctive styles—the front-button cardigan, in either a coat or closer-fitting jacket design, and the more familiar pullover. The cardigan included six or seven "pearl" buttons purchased from a Boston department store.[20] Sweater pockets were optional and added thirty cents to the purchase price for the additional knitting and hand stitching involved. The jacket sweater, offered in the 1910 Canterbury fancy goods catalog, was modeled after the original hand-knit Shaker sweater, "the ones we sisters wore to begin with before we got to using what they call the coat sweater. They were little, snug sweaters, and we had to wear them under what we call the capes of our dress," recalled Sister Ethel Hudson (1896 – 1992), the last Canterbury Sister and the last to have been involved in the sweater industry.[21]

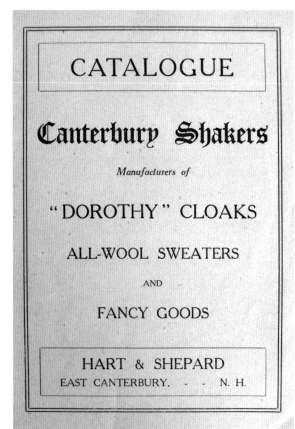

CATALOGUE

Canterbury Shakers

Manufacturers of

"DOROTHY" CLOAKS

ALL-WOOL SWEATERS

AND

FANCY GOODS

HART & SHEPARD
EAST CANTERBURY, - - N. H.

Catalog
Black ink on white paper.
6" x 4 ⅜"; ca. 1910
Canterbury Shaker Village, NH
Canterbury Shaker Village, NH

Catalog Interior
Black ink on white paper.
8¾" x 6"; ca. 1910
Canterbury Shaker Village, NH
Canterbury Shaker Village, NH

SWEATERS

	No. 0	No. 1	No. 2	No. 3
Jacket Sweaters	$7.50	$6.50	$5.70	$4.70
Sweaters	6.50	5.75	5.00	4.25
Pockets, extra				.30
Auto Collar, extra				1.00

COLORS.

Harvard Red	Navy Blue	Dartmouth Green
Gray	Black	White

All sweaters involved a combination of machine knitting and hand stitching, known as "needling." They came in eleven sizes, thirty through fifty, and in each of the four yarn weights. The sleeves and torso to the armpits were knit by machine in a uniform "stockinette" stitch. The 1½-inch hemmed waist and ribbed cuffs were produced by a combination of circular knitting for the sleeves and flat knitting for the upper front and back. The tubular body was divided into right and left sides, with a hand-knit placket covering the raw edges.

Variations occurred in the collar designs. Simplest of all was the V-neck collar with a hand

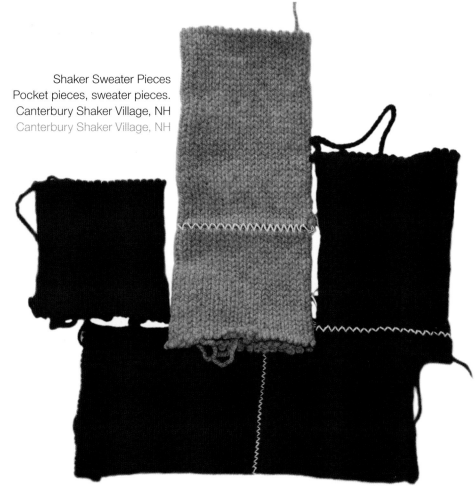

Shaker Sweater Pieces
Pocket pieces, sweater pieces.
Canterbury Shaker Village, NH
Canterbury Shaker Village, NH

Turtleneck Sweater
Red wool.
33" x 19"; First Quarter 20th C.
Canterbury Shaker Village, NH
Canterbury Shaker Village, NH

knit neckband and a placket knit with smaller gauge needles. The rectangular, rib-knit "Military" stand-up collar was made in a single section and hand stitched onto the sweater front. With a single central button, the Military style was modeled after World War I fashions in a newer pattern designed specifically for women. The "auto" collar, for men, was made in three sections of double thickness, outfitted with buttons and loops, and sewn together to form a wide, bulky shawl that either hugged the neck or lay flat along the shoulders.

Finally, and perhaps the best known of the Shaker sweater styles because it sold so well to various colleges: the pullover turtleneck sweater favored by rowers and other athletes. Indeed, the Shakers were the sole suppliers of these sweaters to Yale, Princeton, Harvard, and Dartmouth. These "letter" sweaters were knit in the Shaker's own modified half-cardigan stitch for a thicker, more substantial fabric, with ribbed turtlenecks, waistbands, and cuffs of heavyweight yarns. No one has yet connected the Shakers' sweater patterns to those available elsewhere at the time.[22]

Sweater pieces were assembled by hand, stitching or "needling" the underarms, shoulders, and pockets, binding the raw edges to create near invisible seams. It appears likely that the Sisters used the Kitchener stitch with a tapestry needle.[23] This was a job for a trained and dexterous seamstress. The process began with winding the yarn onto spools every Monday in the knitting room.[24] In conversation with former Curator of Collections at Canterbury Shaker Village Mary Boswell, Sister Ethel Hudson recalled her introduction to the sweater industry as follows: "Well, to begin the first thing I learned to do was wind the yarn. On a Monday I would stand and wind the yarn for three knitters all day."[25] For this task, the Sisters used a 12-spindle winder, purchased in 1887 from the Mayo Machine Company in Lynn, Massachusetts, and powered by the wood-burning stove in the laundry.[26] After assembling eight to ten sweaters, the Sisters carried them in a basket to the North Family.

The North Family had its own industries and was paid extra to make buttonholes, with Sister Hudson assisted by Sisters Alice Howland (1884–1973) who was in charge.[27] They used "a special type of wedge-shaped chisel ('buttonhole scissors') to split the web."[28] They

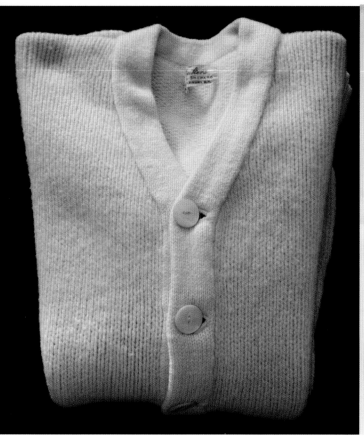

Cardigan Sweater
White wool and mother-of-pearl.
25" x 19"; First Quarter 20th C.
Canterbury Shaker Village, NH
Canterbury Shaker Village, NH

Cardigan Sweater
Gray wool and black buttons.
28" x 21"; First Quarter 20th C.
Canterbury Shaker Village, NH
Canterbury Shaker Village, NH

bound the edges by hand using Corticelli silk thread, a premier thread made by the Corticelli Silk Company, founded in Florence, Massachusetts in 1838.[29] Years later, Sister Hudson described the process to Mary Boswell this way:

> **EH** – We would mark the places where the buttonholes were and then we would stitch them around where they were marked.
>
> **MB** – Would you stitch them by hand?
>
> **EH** – No. On a machine. . . After they were stitched around a half an inch apart we would have buttonhole scissors and cut a slit right between the stitching for the buttonhole. Then we overcast them.
>
> **MB** – And how would you do that? By hand?
>
> **EH** – Yes, and then we made the buttonhole with the buttonhole stitch. And we made the buttonhole with pure silk. We made all the buttonholes. The church sisters would bring up big basketfuls of sweaters for us to make buttonholes.[30]

Sales went exceedingly well. The Sisters found a wholesale outlet for their sweaters through Charles Dudley, a middleman from Hanover, New Hampshire, and had retail sales at sporting goods houses.[31] Swearers were on display in the gift shop at Canterbury and some Sisters made sales trips to resorts around New England or scheduled shows in Philadelphia, New York City, and Washington, D.C. In 1910, for example, Sister Jessie Evans reported a staggering "1489 sweaters made this year."[32]

Work continued apace. Canterbury Sister Josephine Wilson (1866–1946) directed the sweater industry during the early decades of the twentieth century.[33] Her diary from 1919 reads like a litany of tireless labor:

> **Oct. 6** Knit all day.
> **Oct. 7** Knit all day
> **Oct. 9** Knit all day
> **Oct. 29** Knit on Dartmouth Sweater
> **Oct. 30** Knit on Dartmouth Sweater
> **Oct. 31** Knit on Dartmouth Sweater
> **Nov. 5** Green yarn came yesterday, knit today.
> **Nov. 6** knit today
> **Nov. 7** knit today
> **Nov. 10** knit on Dartmouth
> **Nov. 11** knit on Dartmouth
> **Nov. 12** knit on Dartmouth
> **Nov. 13** express team to Concord for yarn.
> **Nov. 14** express team to Concord for yarn. [34]

According to the Canterbury catalogue of 1910, jacket sweater prices ranged from $4.70 to $7.50, depending on the weight of the wool. Pockets added to the cost, as did the auto collar, for which they charged an extra dollar. The cost for a pullover sweater ran from $4.25 to $6.50.[35] While no records remain to show the cost of making a single sweater, Sister Josephine Wilson "records that 100 pounds of white sweater yarn cost $2.05 in 1923."[36] Although the Canterbury Sisters produced only men's sweaters, women occasionally purchased these sweaters for themselves (after all, the so-called "Military" collar was apparently designed with women in mind), as this letter responding to an inquiry from Emma C. Bogat of Jefferson, New Hampshire, implies:

> In reply to your inquiry about sweaters we beg to say we do not make
> ladies [sic] sweaters. Our trade is strictly "mens [sic] sweaters," though in a
> few cases ladies have bought theirs when a loose garment is wanted.[37]

For hand-knit sweaters, women might apply to the Sabbathday Lake Sisters in New Gloucester, Maine. Slower to make, and ordered on an individual basis rather than in bulk, those sweaters cost between ten and sixteen dollars each. Sabbathday Lake Sister Ada S. Cummings (1862–1926) listed and detailed her progress on the sweaters she knit for women in 1910. In the records from this Community, the following may be found:

[1910]

Oct. 21 *I finished off two more white sweaters for Mrs. McCormick.*
   Oct. 24 *I knit a whole front to the green sweater.*
   Oct. 26 *I finished knitting the green sweater: We bought woolen goods from a man who came from the Oxford Mills I begin to knit brown sweater sleeves get one pair partly done.*
   Oct. 27 *I finish knitting both sleeves to brown sweater and barely take up the back tonight.*
   Nov. 3 *Finish knitting brown sweater from 8-fold yarn.*
   Nov. 5 *I work button holes on the brown sweater have bad luck as it was so thick it pushed against the plate and broke my needles.*
   Nov. 11 *Had another pound of green yarn to be sure of enough Mrs. Richardson's....* [38]

COMPETITION AND TRADEMARK CHALLENGES

It is the duty of those at the source of the knit goods industry to supply the wedge with which to pry open the lid of repeat orders. That wedge is the trademark.[39]

CANTERBURY SHAKER VILLAGE was the hub of the sweater industry, with the Communities at Sabbathday Lake, Maine, and Enfield, New Hampshire, participating to a lesser extent. By 1890, the Canterbury Trustees Emeline Hart (1834–1914) and Lucy Shepard (1836–1926) had founded the Hart and Shepard Textile Company, selling cloaks, wool stockings, yarn dust mops, and sweaters to the public under the Hart & Shepard label. For sweaters, an attached silk label read: "Shaker Sweater/Hart and Shepard/E. Canterbury, N.H." In 1901, Sisters Hart and Shepard registered the name "Shaker Sweater" with the state of New Hampshire for a trademark to protect the name from imitators and, in 1902, added the words "The Original" to the label.[40]

[1902]

Trademark for sweaters during the month of August, a trademark was secured by registration to protect our sweater industry. "The Original" will appear hereafter on all marketable garments manufactured by Hart and Shephard.[41]

Obtaining a trademark for the Hart and Shepard label with the federal government proved to be more difficult. In 1908, their application was turned down because the Canterbury Sisters were not able to claim exclusive use of the term "Shaker sweater" for the previous ten years. Unfortunately, the success of the product had made it vulnerable to imitation and copycat merchandising in a competitive marketplace. As a result, the Shaker name was picked up and used liberally by non-Shaker clothing manufacturers, including the Highland Shaker Sweater Company of Camden, New Jersey. They said of themselves: "Manufacturers of pure worsted Shaker sweater coats," and ran ads that claimed: "Our line consists of Pure wool Shaker sweater coat styles, V neck, Byron collars, and shawl collars at attractive prices to the jobbing trade."[42] Likewise, six years later, an article in *Sweater News* entitled, "Summer Sweaters Sell Well in Portland, Oregon" suggests that by 1920, the designation "shaker sweater" had become a generic term:

> One outstanding feature of the past fall and winter season here in the matter of sales was the college shaker sweater for men and boys. Nearly every store, large and small had a call for and did a good business in this style garment.[43]

Two other companies—both of New York City—adopted the Shaker name for their own: Saulter Knitting Mills, which called itself "manufacturers of Shaker sweaters," and Starr's Shaker Sweaters. Such pirating of the Shaker name undermined Sisters Emeline Hart and Lucy Shepard's attempts to obtain a trademark from the U.S. Patent Office in Washington, D.C. The story, recorded in the Family Journal, East Canterbury, unfolded over the course of two years (1907 to 1909):

> **[1907]**
> **On Feb. 28** we signed registration papers for "Shaker Sweaters," our trademark applied for through A.P. Greely, our patent lawyer, Washington, D.C.[44]

> **[1908]**
> **Dec. 2** word from our lawyer was received that the court has decided that we cannot register the words "Shaker Sweaters," unless able to prove ourselves exclusive owners to the trademark for ten years or more. A case similar to ours had been decided, and we're advised to withdraw to prevent a lawsuit. No further explanation given, although it appeared that other parties had been using our trademark.[45]

> **[1909]**
> **Feb. 6** we received from manufacturers, first lot of new trademarks for Shaker Sweaters, unregistered, simply worded "Hart and Shepard – Shakers."

Although defeated in our attempt to secure the words "Shaker Sweaters," our trade will probably continue as heretofore.[46]

The trademark law of 1905 protected the dignity and character of a permanent property, penalized illegal use of a company's logo or brand name, and recognized interstate commerce for the first time in this country.

A trademark is as valuable today as it was in the early twentieth century. Trademarking with the U.S. Patent Office protects a company's brand name, logo, or symbol from wholesale use by competitors seeking to substitute items of inferior workmanship for the original. The trademark acts as a guarantee of quality, assuming the original was made with excellent workmanship and materials; and it encourages the kind of faith in a product (and its label) that garners repeat orders. Unfortunately, once rival manufacturers such as the Highland Sweater Company and others had appropriated the Shaker name, the Sisters could not claim it for their own or protect it from misuse.

Sweater Box Label
Highland Sweater Company
Black and gold ink on paper.
8¾" x 3⅛"; ca. 1910.
Non-Shaker manufacturer, Camden, NJ
Private Collection

END OF AN INDUSTRY

Our trade increased and our business continued to grow and prosper, so long as we were able to get the yarn.[47]

THE SHAKER'S SWEATER INDUSTRY survived for another fifteen years, until 1923, when the Sisters encountered a scarcity of the high-quality Australian wool they had used from the start. Two years earlier, the Shakers had encountered difficulty obtaining a new Lamb knitting machine. As Sister Josephine Wilson wrote in her diary in 1921, "Eldress Mary and Freda go to Chicopee [Massachusetts] by auto with [Brother] Irving [Greenwood (1876–1939)] to test out our knitting machine ordered about 2 years ago. The party returned from Chicopee as they find our machine has been sold. This closes our business with the Lamb Knitting Co!" Lack of high-quality yarn and a suitable knitting machine brought the sweater trade to an abrupt halt.[48] Although reputable clothing manufacturers continue to make and sell items marketed as "Shaker sweaters," these bear little if any resemblance to the original.

12

LATER TWENTIETH CENTURY SHAKER FANCY GOODS

Michael S. Graham, Director,
The Sabbathday Lake Shaker Museum and Library

IMMEDIATELY FOLLOWING the great financial success realized by the Shakers in the 1910s and 1920s from the sale of fancy goods, the Great Depression suddenly collapsed the marketplace just when the Shakers membership went into steep decline. By 1938, all but four of the former Shaker Villages had closed. Then Mount Lebanon followed suit in 1947 and Hancock in 1959. Canterbury dissolved in 1969, when the last Shaker Sister, Ethel Hudson, died there in 1992. Naturally, the production of Shaker fancy goods proportionally declined at each of these Shaker Villages as they neared their end with the exception of the one Community that persevered – Sabbathday Lake Shaker Village.

After the collapse of the tourist-based economy in the 1930s, the Sabbathday Lake Shakers began to serve local audiences and niche markets with a streamlined selection of fancy goods and an emerging, lucrative production of jellies, jams, pickles and relishes, hand-dipped chocolates, and sewn and knit goods. Unlike earlier times when the Maine Shakers employed techniques of specialization and mass-production among teams of Sisters and Brothers to produce upwards of 4,000 pieces of poplarware during the winter season, the ongoing Shaker fancy goods trade after the Depression was in the hands of individuals, or small groups, each of whom shouldered the continuation of their respective crafts and trades. Guided by demand, annual production was streamlined to a fraction of its former heyday. From the mid-20th century on, the production of fancy goods varied according to changes in Shaker membership, such as the arrival of new members, deaths, and defections.

When Brother Delmer Wilson closed the Shakers' mill in 1942, the Sisters continued to produce about 1,000 pieces of poplarware annually before the supply of poplar shavings was entirely depleted by 1945. Despite increasing competition from cheap Asian imports flooding the marketplace and decreasing income from the sale of Shaker fancy goods, the

Sisters continued to produce a selection of silk-lined boxes through the late 1960s. These were clad in Naugahyde and later, off-white or silver synthetic upholstery material, obtained from Montgomery Ward, as well as Porteous & Brawn in Portland, Maine. The production of pincushions, emeries, scissor sheaths, and various styles of mending and sewing kits continued through the late 1970s. The last Shaker cloak, a custom order sewn nearly 20 years after the close of the business, was made by Sister Elsie McCool in 1978.

In the 1980s, "country" and "primitive" decorating styles exploded in popularity, resulting in a surge of interest in "all things Shaker." Unfortunately, usable cottage crafts made by the Shakers were largely superseded by traditional handcrafted woodenware—oval boxes, peg boards, and replica furniture made and designed by non-Shakers for the collector's market. Through the 1980s and into the present day, the range of Shaker fancy goods has included a limited selection and intermittent production of potholders, clothespin bags, oval boxes, Shaker dressed-dolls, pincushions, emeries, knit scarves, ornamental wreaths, woven rag rugs and wool table runners, ash splint baskets, small pieces of woodenware, sewn goods, stuffed toys, letter-press souvenirs from the Shaker Press, and crafts commissioned by the Shakers from craftspeople. Many of these crafts are illustrated in the chapter that follows.

In keeping with their long-standing tradition of sales trips, the Shakers in recent decades have regularly participated in major multi-day events in Maine such as the Common Ground Fair in Unity and the Flower Show in Portland, reaching tens of thousands of people at each event. However, the bulk of their goods are sold on-site at the Shaker Store and the Shaker Museum Visitors' Center, between May and December. Capping the end of each season, the annual Shaker Christmas Fair has been held at the Shaker Store the first Saturday in December for more than 40 years. Today, the fair draws in excess of a thousand shoppers in just five hours, making it the single-most successful retail event of the Shakers' calendar year.

The Community, along with its neighbors, produces small batches of ever-changing novelties and seasonal items for this one-day event. These include sewn and knit goods, handmade Christmas ornaments, small woodenwares, ornamental wreaths, jams and preserves, stuffed dates and sugared nuts, the latter from a nineteenth-century Shaker recipe. There are also freshly baked breads, herbal biscuits, and fruitcakes. Finally, there are always a selection of handcrafted soap and candles, plus the usual array of homemade pickles, dried culinary herbs packed in tins, and the perennial best-selling product: Shaker rosewater in bottles.

True to their progressive and modern approach, the Shakers also have an online store through their website (maineshakers.com) that offers a full selection of their goods to national and international customers year round. The Community has sold its culinary herbs, teas, potpourri, and bottled flavorings on the Internet since the 1990s. Online store sales have steadily increased each year and these currently account for about twenty percent of the earned annual revenue at Shaker Village.

INDEX OF SHAKER NAMES

(appearing in the text)

Mother Ann Lee	1736–1784	Watervliet, NY
Eldress Bertha Lindsay	1897–1990	Canterbury, NH
Aurielia Mace	1835–1910	Sabbathday Lake, ME
Sister Jennie Mathers	1879–1946	Sabbathday Lake, ME
Sister Elsie McCool	1900–1993	Sabbathday Lake, ME
Father Joseph Meacham	1742–1796	Mount Lebanon, NY
Brother Granville Merrill	1839–1878	Sabbathday Lake, ME
Eldress Emma Jane Neale	1847–1943	Mount Lebanon, NY
Sister Sadie Neale	1849–1948	Watervliet, ML, Hancock, MA
Eldress Mary Elizabeth "Lizzie" Noyes	1845–1926	Sabbathday Lake, ME
Brother William Perkins	1861–1934	Mount Lebanon, NY
Sister Bertha Lillian Phelps	1876–1973	Canterbury, NH
Sister Cora Helena Sarle	1867–1956	Canterbury, NH
Elder Otis Sawyer	1815–1884	Sabbathday Lake, ME
Sister Florinda Sears	1825–1901	Mount Lebanon
Sister Lucy Shepard	1836–1926	Canterbury, NH
Sister Rachel Simpson	Unknown	Mount Lebanon, NY
Sister Sarah Ann Standish	1805–1895	Mount Lebanon, NY
Sister Rosetta Stephens	1860–1948	Mount Lebanon, NY
Sister Prudence A. Stickney	1860–1950	Sabbathday Lake, ME
Sister Jennie Wells	1878–1956	Mount Lebanon, Hancock, MA
Eldress Lois Wentworth	1824–1897	Many Villages then to Hancock, MA
Sister Martha Wetherell	1855–1944	Mount Lebanon, NY; Enfield, NH; Canterbury, NH
Brother Delmer Wilson	1873–1961	Sabbathday Lake, ME
Sister Josephine Wilson	1866–1946	Canterbury, NH
Sister Mary Ann Wilson	1863–1944	Canterbury, NH
Mother Lucy Wright	1760–1821	Watervliet, NY?
Brother Isaac Newton Youngs	1793–1865	New Lebanon, NY

FURTHER READINGS

Edward D. Andrews, *The Community Industries of the Shakers;* Reprint of New York State Museum Handbook 15, 1933 (Charlestown, MA: Emporium Publications, 1971).

Mary Rose Boswell, "Women's Work: The Canterbury Shakers' Fancywork Industry." *Historical New Hampshire, Special Issue, Canterbury Shaker Village* (Concord, NH: New Hampshire Historical Society, vol. 48. nos. 2 & 3: Summer/Fall 1993).

Wendy E. Chmielewski, Louis J. Kern, and Marlyn Klee-Hartzell, editors, *Women in Spiritual and Communitarian Societies in the United States,* "Shaker Fancy Goods: Women's Work and Presentation of Self in the Community Context in the Victorian Era." Beverly Gordon (Syracuse, NY: Syracuse University Press, 1993).

Beverly Gordon, *Shaker Textile Arts* (Hannover, NH, and London: University Press of New England, 1980).

Beverly Gordon, "Victorian Fancy Goods, Another Reappraisal of Shaker Material Culture." Winterthur Portfolio: vol. 25 no. 2/3: Summer/Autumn (Chicago: University of Chicago Press, 1990).

Michael S Graham; Daniel W. Patterson; Gerard C. Wertkin; Arnold S. Hadd; Frances A, Carr, *The Human and the Eternal: Shaker Art in its Many Forms* (United Society of Shakers: Sabbathday Lake, Inc., New Gloucester, ME: 2009).

Gerrie Kennedy, Galen Beal, Jim Johnson, "The Shaker Poplarware Industry." *Shaker Baskets and Poplarware, A Field Guide,* vol. III (Stockbridge, MA: Berkshire House, 1982).

M. Stephen Miller, *Inspired Innovations: A Celebration of Shaker Ingenuity* (Hanover and London: University Press of New England, 2010).

M. Stephen Miller, *From Shaker Lands and Shaker Hands: A Survey of the Industries* (Hanover and London: University Press of New England, 2007).

June Sprigg, *By Shaker Hands* (Hanover, NH: University Press of New England, 1990).

Stephen J. Stein, *The Shaker Experience in America: A History of the United Society of Believers* (New Haven and London: Yale University Press, 1992).

Scott Swank, *Shaker Life, Art, and Architecture* (New York, London, Paris: Abbeville Press Publishers, 1999).

Gerard C. Wertkin, *The Four Seasons of Shaker Life* (New York, NY: Simon & Schuster, Inc., 1986).

Martha Wetherbee and Nathan Taylor, *Shaker Baskets* (Martha Wetherbee Basket Shop, 1988).

CATALOGS:

Catalog of Fancy Goods Made at Shaker Village Alfred, York County, Maine, 1908.

Catalog of Fancy Goods Made by the Shakers, Sabbathday Lake, Maine, 1910.

Products of Intelligence and Diligence, Shakers Church Family, Mount Lebanon Col. Co., New York, 1908.

Brother Theodore E. Johnson, *Ingenious and Useful, Shaker Sisters Communal Industries, 1860-1960.*

NOTES

INTRODUCTION: SHAKER FANCY GOODS

1 Sabbathday Lake, ME, Church Record and Journal, vol. 4, 1890-1897.

2 The Journal of Sister Aurelia Mace, Sabbathday Lake, ME, 14-DJ-120.

3 Mary Rose Boswell, "Women's Work: The Canterbury Shakers' Fancywork Industry," *Historic New Hampshire, Special Issue, Canterbury Shaker Village,* Vol. 48, Nos. 2 & 3 (Summer/Fall 1993), 150-151.

4 Ibid., 134.

5 With the increased productivity of the Industrial Revolution came a much higher standard of living, which may have helped create a market for Shaker fancy goods among those, increasing in number, who could afford novel items of quality workmanship. "Economic Growth in the Early Industrial Revolution," *U.S. History Online Textbook Program,* ushistory.org/us/22a.asp.

6 Ibid., 148.

7 John Kirk, *The Shaker World, Art, Life, Belief* (New York: Harry N. Abrams, Inc., 1997), 211-213.

8 Ibid., 217.

9 Stephen J. Stein, *The Shaker Experience in America, A History of the United Society of Believers* (New Haven: Yale University Press, 1992), 269.

10 Stein, "South Family Events by Anna Goepper, 10-11 Dec. 1912," *The Shaker Experience in America* (New Haven: Yale University Press, 1992), 269.

11 The Journal of Sister Aurelia Mace, Sabbathday Lake, ME, 14-DJ-120.

12 June Sprigg, *By Shaker Hands* (Hanover, NH: University Press of New England, 1990), 10.

13 Gerard C. Wertkin, "Settling Down," in *Four Seasons of Shaker Life, An Intimate Portrait of the Community at Sabbathday Lake* (New York: Simon & Schuster, 1986), 54.

14 Jennie Mathers's Diary, Sabbathday Lake, ME, 1920.

15 Wertkin, *Four Seasons of Shaker Life,* 54.

16 Bertha Lindsay, "Industries and Inventions, A Brief History," Canterbury Shakers.

17 Church Record and Journal, Sabbathday Lake, ME, vol. 4, 1890-1897.

18 Church Record and Journal, Sabbathday Lake, ME, vol. 4, 1890-1897.

19 *Brooklyn Daily Eagle,* Brooklyn, NY, August 22, 1866.

20 *Nebraska State Journal,* June 26, 1922.

21 "Concerning the Memorial Pres. Church Fair," *Brooklyn Daily Eagle,* Brooklyn, NY, Dec 9, 1869.

22 Sabbathday Lake Church Record and Journal, vol. 4, 1890-1897.

23 This letter is edited and annotated by Richard Cary in *Sarah Orne Jewett Letters;* the manuscript is held by Colby College Special Collections, Waterville, ME.

24 Jewett refers here to the Shaker community at Alfred, ME first settled by Shakers in 1783; made an official community with the building of a meeting house ten years later.

25 From *the Hill-Top*, no. 3, The Poland Springs Hotel, Poland Springs, ME, July 19, 1896.

26 Jewett, Ibid.

27 Church Record and Journal, 1898-1906, 14-DJ-040.

28 Jennie Mathers' Diary, Sabbathday Lake, ME, 1920.

29 Jennie Mathers' Diary, Sabbathday Lake, ME, 1920.

30 "Novelties from Shaker Land. Annual Sale for the Benefit of the East Canterbury Community," *Boston Daily Globe*, Boston, MA, Dec. 6, 1899.

31 Draws the People— Crowds Attend Mechanic Fair- Recently Arrived Exhibits, *Boston Daily Globe*, Boston, MA, Oct. 15, 1890.

32 Sabbathday Lake Church Record and Journal 1898-1906, 14-DJ-040.

33 Otis Sawyer, "Otis Sawyer in Account," Sabbathday Lake, ME. 1896-1906, 14-FR 090.

34 Jennie Mathers' Diary, Sabbathday Lake, ME, 1920.

35 The Journal of Sister Aurelia Mace, Sabbathday Lake, ME, 14-DJ-120.

36 Stein, *The Shaker Experience in America* (New Haven: Yale University Press, 1992), 270.

37 Martha M. Libster, *A History of Shaker Nurse Herbalists, Health Reform, and the American Botanical Movement* (1830-1860), Journal of Holistic Nursing 2009 27: 222 originally published online 11 August 2009, 229.

CHAPTER 1: PENWIPES

1 Vol 4 Sabbathday Lake, ME, Church Record and Journal 1890 – 1897

2 Edward D. Andrews, *The Community Industries of the Shakers* (Reprint of New York State Museum Handbook 15 by Emporium Publications: 1933) 44.

3 Andrews, 168.

4 Andrews, 44.

5 Beverly Gordon, Chapter 6, "Fancywork" in *Shaker Textile Arts* (University Press of New England, Hanover and London: 1980) 238.

6 Interview with Charles "Bud" Thompson (conducted 9/20/17).

7 Sharon Duane Koomler, "Shaker Textiles Cloak Making," Chapter 7 of *Inspired Innovations, A Celebration of Shaker Ingenuity*, M. Stephen Miller (University Press of New England, Hanover and London: 2010) 109.

8 14-FR-260 1930 undated journal thought to have been written in 1930.

9 *Victorian Penwipers and Blotters*, originally published in 1874 and 1899, copyright @ 2009 Dakota Prairie Treasures.

10 Michael S Graham; Daniel W Patterson; Gerard C Wertkin; Arnold S Hadd; Frances A Carr, *The Human and the Eternal: Shaker Art in its Many Forms* (United Society of Shakers: Sabbathday Lake, Inc., New Gloucester, ME: 2009), 59.

11 70Ac3v..9 Williams College Special Collections, Mount Lebanon Journal. 37.

12 Koomler, 109.

13 Records kept by the Church at Mount Lebanon, Vol IV, August 1871, 10.343.

14 Sabbathday Lake Account book 1927-1943 #1315.

15 *Canterbury Shakers, Manufacturers of "Dorothy" Cloaks, Men's All-Wool Sweaters, Fancy Goods and Medicines,* Hart and Shephard, East Canterbury, NH, 2nd and 3rd editions, early 20th Century.

16 *Hart and Shephard, Manufacturers of Athletic and Fancy Goods Holiday Goods Specialty Shakers,* East Canterbury, NH, 1st edition, early 20th Century.

CHAPTER 2: EMERIES, PINCUSHIONS, AND NEEDLE BOOKS

1 https://www.ngv.vic.gov.au/the-sewing-needle-a-history-through-16-19th-centuries, accessed March 2018.

2 Emery is finely ground corundum (aluminum oxide), an extremely hard mineral used chiefly as an abrasive.

3 Otis Sawyer, Sabbathday Lake, ME, 1875-1951.

4 Catalog of Fancy Goods, Made by the Shakers, Sabbathday Lake, ME, 1910.

5 Detroit Free Press, Detroit, MI, Sun., Jan. 24, 1915, 77.

6 Mary Rose Boswell, "Women's Work: The Canterbury Shakers' Fancywork Industry," *Historical New Hampshire, Special Issue, Canterbury Shaker Village,* (Concord, NH: New Hampshire Historical Society, Vol. 48. Nos. 2 & 3: Summer/Fall 1993), 132-154.

7 Records kept by the church at Mount Lebanon, vol. IV, 10:343.

8 WRHS-VB-v217, Fruitlands, Harvard, MA.

9 Journal of Anna Dodgson, Mount Lebanon, NY, 1873-1879.

10 Jennie Mathers' Diary, Sabbathday Lake, ME, 1920.

11 Jennie Mathers' Diary, Sabbathday Lake, ME, 1921.

12 *The Independent Record*, Helena, MT, Sun., Nov. 14, 1954, p. 201.

13 Gay Ann Rodgers, *An Illustrated History of Needlework Tools* (London: John Murray Publishing Ltd., 1983), 152.

14 Helen Lester Thompson, *Sewing Tools and Trinkets* (Paducah, KY: Collector Books, Division of Schroeder Publishing, 1997), 83.

15 An Account of Work Performed by Sisters in the Church Commencing January 1, 1872, for sale, 1872-1894.

16 Mrs. Olive Socklixis, Old Towne, ME, letter to the Canterbury Shakers, Hart and Shepard, March 30th, 1943. Located at the Mount Kearsarge Indian Museum, Warner, NH.

17 Conversation with Michael Graham, Director, Sabbathday Lake, New Gloucester, ME.

18 Journal, Anna Dodgson, 1873-1879.

19 Mount Lebanon Church, Records kept by the Church at Mount Lebanon, vol. IV, 108.343.

20 Can-Fin 1927-1943 Book 1 Sales Records Canterbury Journal, (315) Canterbury, NH.

21 Can-Fin 1944-1971 Book 2 Sales Records Canterbury Journal, (790) Canterbury, NH.

22 Josephine E. Wilson Diary, 1928, 1985.61, Canterbury, NH.

CHAPTER 3: CORA HELENA SARLE – BOTANICAL ARTIST AND FANCY GOODS PAINTER

1 June Sprigg, Introduction to *A Shaker Sister's Drawings, Wild Plants Illustrated,* by Cora Helena Sarle (New York, NY: Monacelli Press, 1997).

2 Scott T. Swank, Afterword to *A Shaker Sister's Drawings, Wild Plants Illustrated,* by Cora Helena Sarle (New York, NY: Monacelli Press, 1997).

3 June Sprigg, Introduction to *A Shaker Sister's Drawings.*

4 https://www.jstor.org/stable/1181214?seq=1#page_scan_tab_contents, Winterthur Portfolio, 1989, Henry Francis duPont Winterthur Museum, Inc. (accessed March 2018).

5 June Sprigg, Introduction to *A Shaker Sister's Drawings.*

6 Correspondence with Darryl Thompson, September 2017.

7 Tape E1, a, b, transcript Jan 29, 1979, interview with Bertha Lindsay.

8 Interview with Charles "Bud" Thompson, September 2017.

9 Darryl Thompson, Ibid.

Chapter 4 Raccoon Fur and Silk Gloves

1 Journal Deaconess Church Family [Mount Lebanon] 1879-1882, Anna Dodgson, 1882.

2 Journal Deaconess Church Family [Mount Lebanon] 1883-1885, Anna Dodgson, 1883.

3 Edward Deming Andrews, *The Community Industries of the Shakers,* Reprint of New York State Museum Handbook 15, 1933 (Charlestown, MA: Emporium Publications, 1971), 80-81.

4 70Ac3v.7 Williams College Special Collections.

5 Shaker Museum, Old Chatham, NY, Object No. 6622. Gifted September 1953. The card states the cap is made of silk and raccoon fur. However, upon inspection, the cap appears to be wool and raccoon fur.

6 Records kept by order of the Church at Mount Lebanon, NY, vol. IV, 10.343, 1879.

7 70Ac3v9 Williams College Special Collections.

8 Records kept by order of the Church at Mount Lebanon, NY, vol. IV, 10.343, 1877.

9 Journal Deaconess Church Family [Mount Lebanon] 1879-1882, Anna Dodgson, 1881.

10 Journal Deaconess Church Family [Mount Lebanon] 1883-1885, Anna Dodgson, 1883.

11 Records kept by order of the Church at Mount Lebanon, NY, vol. IV, 10.343, 1884.

12 Edward Deming Andrews, 252.

13 Sister Mary Hazard's (1811-1899) brother owned a mill in Hancock where the Sisters and Brethren took the fur and silk to be carded. (Conversation with Jerry Grant, Director of Collections and Research, Shaker Museum Old Chatham, NY. May 2018).

14 Records kept by order of the Church at Mount Lebanon, NY, vol. IV, 10.343. 1878.

15 Records kept by order of the Church at Mount Lebanon, NY, vol. IV, 10.343. 1879.

16 Records kept by order of the Church at Mount Lebanon, NY, vol. IV, 10.343. 1880.

17 Edward Deming Andrews, 252.

18 Records kept by order of the Church at Mount Lebanon, NY, vol. IV, 10.343. 1880.

19 Records kept by order of the Church at Mount Lebanon, NY, vol. IV, 10.343. 1884.

20 *The Inner Ocean*, Chicago, Illinois, October 15, 1887.

21 70Ac3v9 Williams College Special Collections, January 16, 1888.

22 *The Inner Ocean*, Chicago, Illinois, 1985.

27 Journal Deaconess Church Family [Mount Lebanon] of Anna Dodgson 1879-1882, 1882.

28 Journal Deaconess Church Family [Mount Lebanon] of Anna Dodgson 1883-1885, 1883.

29 Records kept by order of the Church Family Mount Lebanon, N.Y., vol. IV 10.343, 1879.

30 Records kept by order of the Church Family Mount Lebanon, N.Y., vol. IV 10.343, 1883.

31 Beverly Gordon, *Shaker Textile Arts* (Hanover, NH and London: University Press of New England, 1980), 43.

32 Records kept by Order of the Church Family at Mount Lebanon, N.Y, vol. IV 10.343

CHAPTER 5 DOLLS

1 14-DJ-040 SDL Church Record and Journal, Sabbath Day Lake Journal.

2 "The Shakers, A Strict and Utopian Way of Life Has Almost Vanished," *LIFE,* March 21, 1949, 142-148.

3 CAN-COR 1936-1949, Canterbury, NH.

4 Sharon Duane Koomler, "Shaker Textiles Cloak Making," in *Inspired Innovations,* M. Stephen Miller (Lebanon, NH: University Press of New England, 2010), 109.

5 *The Brooklyn Daily Eagle,* Brooklyn, NY, Tuesday December 5, 1911, page 2.

6 14-FR-090 1869-1906 Otis Sawyer in Account, Sabbathday Lake Journal.

7 Ibid.

8 *Catalog of Fancy Goods made by the Shakers,* Sabbathday Lake, ME, 1910.

9 *Products of Intelligence and Diligence,* Shakers Church Family, Mount Lebanon Col. Co., NY, 1908.

10 *The Brooklyn Daily Eagle,* Brooklyn, NY, Tuesday December 5, 1911, page 2..

11 Ibid.

12 Ibid.

13 CAN-FIN 1929-1943. Canterbury Journal.

CHAPTER 6 THE SHAKER CLOAK

1 14-DJ-040 Church Record and Journal Sabbathday Lake, ME (1898-1906).

2 Anna Marie Greaves' Journal 7224 #56 Mount Lebanon, NY.

3 Beverly Gordon, *Shaker Textile Arts* (Hanover and London: University Press of New England, 1980), 152-153.

4 Ibid., 185.

5 Ibid.

6 Stephen J. Paterwic, *Historical Dictionary of the Shakers* (Lanham, MD; Toronto, Oxford: 2008), 160-161.

7 From the Introduction to the fancy goods catalogue, *Products of Intelligence and Diligence,* Shaker Church Family, Mount Lebanon Col. Co., New York, 1908.

8 Cloaks shipped 10415 # 104 Mount Lebanon, NY.

9 A handwritten form letter to customers sent out on Mount Lebanon stationary and signed by Eldress Emma J. Neale, shown here as it appeared in *The Shaker Cloak,* a brochure printed and distributed by the Shakers at Mount Lebanon, NY, in 1915.

10 Sharon Duane Koomler, "Shaker Textiles Cloaking Making," chapter 7 of *Inspired Innovations, A Celebration of Shaker Ingenuity,* by M. Stephen Miller (Hanover and London: University Press of New England, 2010), 107-109.

11 Koomler, 108. The Russell Woolen Mill was built by the four Russell brothers in 1863, making its founders a fortune by supplying Union soldiers with uniforms and blankets, according to "S.N. & C. Russell Manufac-

turing," *The Mills of Pittsfield, Our Cultural History*, https://milltour.org/2014/06/26/s-n-c-russell-manufacturing/ 2014 (accessed June 27, 2018).

12 Koomler, 108.

13 Cat. No 8906 1901, Mount Lebanon, NY.

14 Koomler, 109.

15 Vol. IV 10.343, Cloaks Shipped, 10415, #104 Mount Lebanon, NY.

16 Ibid.

17 Anna Marie Greaves' Journal 7224 #56., Mount Lebanon, NY.

18 Cloaks shipped 10415 #104 Mount Lebanon, NY.

19 Martin Gregory, *ISMACS News* Issue 93. "The Gem" was patented in America on April 25, 1899, and subsequently in Canada, Europe, and Russia, between 1899 and 1903.

20 Koomler, 107-109.

21 Scott Swank, *Shaker Life, Art, and Architecture* (New York, London, Paris: Abbeville Press Publishers, 1999), 195-196.

22 Family Journal or Current Events Compiled and Transcribed by Jessie Evans et al, 1901 to 1915, Church Family, East Canterbury, NH.

23 M. Stephen Miller, *Inspired Innovations, A Celebration of Shaker Ingenuity* Miller (Hanover and London: University Press of New England, 2010), 110.

24 Swank, 196.

25 Koomler, 111.

26 Gordon, 185.

27 Miller, 110

28 Gordon, 247.

29 CAN/DJ Canterbury, NH, Journal Manuscript.

30 *Evening Star*, Washington, D.C., Thursday, December 14, 1905 (downloaded March 22, 2016).

31 Family Journal or Current Events compiled and transcribed by Jessie Evans, et al., 1901 to 1915, Church Family, East Canterbury, NH.

32 Ibid.

33 *Catalog of Fancy Goods Made by the Shakers*, Sabbathday Lake, ME, 1910. Italics added.

34 Eldress Elizabeth "Lizzie" Noyes was known for her unflagging engagement in the manufacturing of fancy goods, her exemplary work ethic. She was appointed Eldress in 1880, at the same time William Dumont was appointed Elder. "Together, they led the community through its golden age of prosperity, 1880-1926," according to Stephen J. Paterwic. For more on Eldress Noyes' dedication and involvement in the Sabbathday Lake community, see Paterwic's *Historical Dictionary of the Shakers* (Lanham, MD; Toronto, Oxford: The Scarecrow Press, Inc., 2008), 160-161.

35 14-DJ-040 Sabbathday Day Lake Church Record and journal.

36 Ibid.

37 14-DJ-040 Sabbathday Day Lake Church Record and journal, 1901.

38 14-DJ-040 Sabbathday Day Lake Church Record and journal, 1902.

39 14-FR-90 1869-1906 Sabbathday Lake Record.

40 *Catalog of Fancy Goods Made by the Shakers,* Sabbathday Lake, ME, 1910.

41 George Henry Green, Trustee letter dated April 6, 1902, Sabbathday Lake.

42 CAN-FIN 1927-1943, Canterbury, NH, Journal.

43 Letter sent to Mrs. John. S. Williams, on stationary with the letterhead, "Canterbury Shakers, East Canterbury, New Hampshire," signed "The Canterbury Shakers, per Emma B. King," and dated Nov. 10, 1948.

44 Accession file card #7904 from the Shaker Museum, Mount Lebanon.

Chapter 7 Shaker Fans

1 Beverly Gordon, "Victorian Fancy Goods, Another Reappraisal of Shaker Material Culture," Winterthur Portfolio Vol. 25, No. 2/3 Summer/Autumn (Chicago: University of Chicago Press, 1990), 118.

2 "The Fascination of the Fan," *Fabrics, Fancy Goods, and Notions,* vol. 45, March 1911, 18.

3 https://www.fancircleinternational.org/history/fans-of-tutankhamuns-tomb. (Accessed April 15, 2018)

4 Esther Oldham, "A Shaker Industry—Fan Making, Part II," *The Antiques Journal,* no. 10 (October 1955): 22-23, 34.

5 Suzanne R. Thurman, *O Sisters Ain't You Happy: Gender, Family, and Community among the Harvard and Shirley Shakers, 1781—1918* (Syracuse: Syracuse University Press: 2002), 75.

6 Brother Theodore E. Johnson, "Ingenious & Useful, Shaker Sisters Communal Industries," 1860-1960. United Society of Shakers, Sabbathday Lake, ME.

7 Deacons Journal Center Family New Lebanon 1848-1857.

8 Fruitlands Manuscript 4.2. Trustees of the Reservations, MA.

9 Brother Theodore E. Johnson.

10 Grove Blanchard Journal 1836-1839, WRHS. Cleveland, OH.

11 Ibid.

12 Ibid.

13 Ibid.

14 Esther Oldham, 22-23, 34.

15 Fruitlands Manuscript 31.4. Trustees of the Reservations, MA.

16 Jerry Grant, "Why did the Shakers Switch from Palm Leaf to Poplar?" https://shakerml.org/why-did-the-shakers-switch-from-palm-leaf-to-poplar/January 24/February 18.

17 M. Stephen Miller, *From Shaker Hands and Shaker Lands* (Hanover and London: University Press of New England, 2007), 149.

Chapter 8 Poplarware Boxes

1 Sabbathday Lake Church Record, vol. 4. 1890-1897, United Society, Sabbathday Lake, ME.

2 Mary Rose Boswell, "Women's Work: The Canterbury Shakers' Fancywork Industry," Historic New Hampshire, Special Issue, Canterbury Shaker Village, vol. 48, nos. 2 & 3 (Concord, New Hampshire: New Hampshire Historic Society, Summer/Fall 1993), 135.

3 Ibid., 135.

4 Gerrie Kennedy, Galen Beal, Jim Johnson, Shaker Baskets & Poplarware: A Field Guide, vol. III (Stockbridge, MA: Berkshire House, 1992), "The Shaker Poplarware Industry," 86-87.

5 Jerry Grant, "Why did the Shakers Switch from palm leaf to poplar?" (https://shakerml.wordpress. com/2018/01/24/why-did-the-shakers-switch-from-palm-leaf-to-poplar/ January 24).

6 Mary Rose Boswell, 136.

7 M. Stephen Miller, From Shaker Lands and Shaker Hands: A Survey of the Industries (Hanover and London: University Press of New England, 2007), 147-148.

8 Jerry Grant, idem.

9 Conversation with Michael Graham, Director, The United Society of Shakers, Sabbathday Lake, ME April 2019.

10 Pearson, Elmer R., Neal, Julia, The Shaker Image, Second and Annotated Edition (Hancock Shaker Village, Inc., 1994). See "Martha Wetherell," 262.

11 Gerrie Kennedy, Galen Beal, Jim Johnson, idem.

12 Sister Elsie McCool, 55-59.

13 Mount Lebanon Journal, 1868 – December 1877. Williams College Special Collections 70Ac3v.7, 43. Williamstown, MA.

14 Church Record and Journal, vol. 4, Sabbathday Lake, June 1894, p. 282. United Society of Shakers, Sabbathday Lake, ME.

15 Sister Elsie McCool, 55-59.

16 Ibid., 55-59.

17 Ibid., 55-59.

18 Church Record and Journal, vol. 4, Sabbathday Lake, ME, 1890-1897, 399. United Society of Shakers, Sabbathday Lake, ME.

19 Sabbathday Lake Journal, 1910-1912, 14-FR-250. United Society of Shakers, Sabbathday Lake, ME.

20 Church Record and Journal, Vol. 4. United Society of Shakers, Sabbathday Lake, ME.

21 Sabbathday Lake Church Record and Journal 1898-1906, 14-DJ-040. United Society of Shakers, Sabbathday Lake, ME.

22 M. Stephen Miller, Inspired Innovations: A Celebration of Shaker Ingenuity (London and Hanover: University Press of New England, 2010), 135-6.

23 Sister Elsie McCool, 55-59.

24 Ibid., 59.

25 James Elliot (pseudonym for Brother Theodore Johnson), "Shaker Collecting," Maine Antique Digest, Vol. II (February 1974), 24-25.

26 Gerrie Kennedy, Beal, Galen, Johnson, Jim, "The Poplarware Industry," Shaker Baskets and Poplarware, A Field Guide, vol. III (Stockbridge, MA: Berkshire House, 1992) 134.

27 Gerrie Kennedy, Galen Beale, and Jim Johnson, 86-89.

28 Gerard C. Wertkin, The Four Seasons of Shaker Life (New York, NY: Simon & Schuster, Inc., 1986) 80-81.

29 Records kept by the Church Family at Mount Lebanon, vol. IV, 10.343, 1877.

30 "Otis Sawyer in Account," 14-FR 090, 1896-1906. United Society of Shakers, Sabbathday Lake, ME.

31 James Elliot, 24-25.

32 Excerpt from tape #24, interview with Eldress Bertha Lindsay (1897–1990), of Canterbury, by Mary Rose Boswell, curator of collections, Canterbury Shaker Village, Canterbury, NH, November, 28, 1983.

33 A Daily Journal of Record of Events Changes to recurring in the community of E. Canterbury, N.H., vol. I, 1893- 1895. 227.

34 Ibid., V. II, 1896- 1899

35 Can-Mem 36 Journal, A Biographical Record of the Church Family at Canterbury, N.H., 1893-vol. II, 4. Canterbury, NH.

36 1890 Can-Dij 29 Canterbury Journal, Canterbury Shaker Village, NH.

37 Brooklyn Daily Eagle, Tuesday, February 27, 1900, 9.

38 [Mss. NO 8851] Mount Lebanon Journal, Shaker Museum I Mount Lebanon, NY.

39 "Orders, Poplar Work," Historical New Hampshire, Special Issue, Canterbury Shaker Village, vol. 48, nos. 2 & 3, (Concord, NH: New Hampshire Historical Society), Summer/Fall. 148.

40 Brother Theodore E. Johnson, Ingenious and Useful: Shaker Sisters' Communal Industries, 1860-1960. (United Society of Shakers, Sabbathday Lake, ME, 1986).

CHAPTER 9 SHAKER BASKETS

1 Martha Wetherbee and Nathan Taylor, *Shaker Baskets* (Sanbornton, NH: Martha Wetherbee Basket Shop. 1988), 85.

2 Conversation with Nathan Taylor, Spring 2020.

3 Ibid.

4 Ibid.

5 Ibid.

6 Martha Wetherbee and Nathan Taylor, *Shaker Baskets,* (Sanbornton, NH: Martha Wetherbee Basket Shop. 1988), 79–84.

7 Conversation with Nathan Taylor, Spring 2020.

8 Ibid.

9 *Lindsay, Industries and Inventions, A Brief History,* Sister Bertha Lindsay, Canterbury Shakers, 1961.

10 Conversation with Nathan Taylor, Spring 2020

11 Wetherbee and Taylor, 86.

12 Conversation with Nathan Taylor, Spring 2020.

13 Ibid.

14 Ibid.

15 Ibid.

16 Ibid.

17 Wetherbee and Taylor, 88.

18 Gerrie Kennedy, Galen Beale, and Jim Johnson, Shaker Baskets and Poplarware: A field Guide, Volume III (Stockbridge, MA: Berkshire House, 1992) 30.

19 Conversation with Nathan Taylor, Spring 2020.

20 Work performed by Sisters First Order 1872 Mount Lebanon 1872-1894, Fruitlands, The Trustees of Reservations, Harvard, MA 6-3.

21 Image from 1874 Records kept by order of the Church Family, Vol. IV, 10.343

22 Wetherbee and Taylor, 80.

23 Ibid, 82.

24 Journal of Anna Dodgson, 1873-1879 (1875 Journal)

25 Records kept by the Church Family at Mount Lebanon, Vol. IV., August 1871, 10.343

26 Journal of Anna Dodgson, 1879-1883.

27 Wetherbee and Taylor, 91.

28 Ibid, 89.

29 Ibid, 89.

Chapter 10 Shaker Fancy Brushes and Dusters

1 14-DJ-120, The Journal of Sister Aurelia Mace, Sabbathday Lake, ME, Feb 6, 1896. United Society of Shakers, Sabbathday Lake, ME.

2 *Testimonies of the Life, Revelations, and Doctrines of Mother Ann Lee* (Second Edition, Albany, N.Y. 1888), 208.

3 Conversation with Kent Ruesswick, Canterbury Brushworks, Canterbury, NH, March 2018.

4 Ibid.

5 Ibid.

6 M. Stephen Miller, *Inspired Innovations, A Celebration of Shaker Ingenuity* (Hanover, NH and London: University Press of New England, 2010), 148.

7 Church Record and Journal, vol. 4, Sabbathday Lake, ME

8 14-FR-090, Otis Sawyer, "Otis Sawyer in Account,"1896-1906. Sabbathday Lake, ME.

9 14-DJ-040, Church Record and Journal, Sabbathday Lake, ME, 1901.

Chapter 11 Shaker Sweaters

1 CAN-D/J Canterbury NH Journal, 1900. Canterbury Shaker Village, NH.

2 Beverly Gordon, *Shaker Textile Arts* (Hanover and London: University Press of New England, 1980), 81.

3 Anon., "About the Shaker Sweater," unpublished modern paper. Canterbury Shaker Village, NH.

4 Josephine E. Wilson Diary, 1918, Canterbury Shaker Village, NH. Cited by Jean M. Burks, 5.

5 Anon., unpublished modern paper. "About the Shaker Sweater." Canterbury Shaker Village, NH.

6 Scott M. Swank, *Shaker Life, Art, and Architecture: Hands to Work, Hearts to God* (New York: Abbeville Publishing Group, 1999), 195.

7 CAN-D/J 29 Canterbury, NH Journal. Canterbury Shaker Village, NH.

8 Burks, 6.

9 Latch needles, patented in France in 1806 and still sold today, have a hook that captures the looped yarn and a latch that secures it.

10 Burks, 6.

11 Ibid.

12 Anon., unpublished modern papers, "History of the Shaker Sweater" and "About the Shaker Sweater," Cited in Swank, idem, 195, and note 20, 217.

13 Swank, 195.

14 Can-D/J 29 Canterbury, NH, Journal, 1890. Canterbury Shaker Village, NH.

15 Can-D/J 29 Canterbury, NH, Journal, 1891. Canterbury Shaker Village, NH.

16 Can-D/J29 Canterbury NH, Journal, 1905. Canterbury Shaker Village, NH.

17 Ibid., 82.

18 Ibid., 78.

19 Anon., "About the Shaker Sweater."

20 Burks, 8.

21 Ethel Hudson interviewed by Mary Boswell, Curator of Collections, Canterbury Shaker Village, 1986.

22 Burks, 7.

23 Barbara Abbey, *The Complete Book of Knitting* (New York: The Viking Press, 1971), 90, cited in Burks, idem., 8.

24 Burks, 7.

25 Ethel Hudson interviewed by Mary Boswell, Curator of Collections, Canterbury Shaker Village, 1986.

26 Burks, 8.

27 Ibid.

28 Ibid.

29 https://www.needlenthread.com/2015/01/corticelli-silk-thread-color-card-with-real-thread-samples.html (accessed October 4, 2018).

30 Ethel Hudson interviewed by Mary Boswell.

31 Burks, 8.

32 CAN-D/J Canterbury NH Journal. Canterbury Shaker Village, NH.

33 Josephine E. Wilson diary, 1919 1985.53 Canterbury Shaker Village, NH.

34 Ibid.

35 *Catalogue Canterbury Manufacturers of "Dorothy" Cloaks, All-Wool Sweaters and Fancy Goods*, Hart & Shepard, East Canterbury, NH, 1910-1920.

36 Josephine E. Wilson Diary, 1923, Shaker Village, Canterbury, NH, cited in Burks, note 16. Canterbury Shaker Village, NH.

37 Letter from the Shakers to Emma C. Bogat, August 29, 1908, Canterbury Shaker Village, NH.

38 Sabbathday Lake, ME, 1910 14-DJ-140 Ada S Cummings' Diary. United Society of Shakers, Sabbathday Lake, ME.

39 Ira A. Schiller, "Why the Trade-Mark is an Asset," published in *Sweater News: The Journal of the Sweater and Fancy Goods Trade*, vol. 1, Dec. 1913, 14.

40 Family Journal of Current Events Compiled and Transcribed by Jessie Evens, et al., 1901–1915, Church Family, East Canterbury, NH Canterbury Shaker Village, NH. 1902.

41 Ibid.

42 *Sweater News: The Journal of the Sweater and Fancy Good Trade*, 320 Broadway, New York, N.Y., Vol. 1, No. 9, August 1914, 22.

43 *Sweater News: The Journal of the Sweater and Fancy Goods Trade*, 320 Broadway, New York, N.Y., Vol 7, No. 6, June 1920, excerpt May 11, 1920.

44 Family Journal of Current Events Compiled and Transcribed by Jessie Evens, et al., 1901–1915, Church Family, East Canterbury, NH, 82. Canterbury Shaker Village, NH.

45 Ibid., 94.

46 Ibid., 106.

47 Anon., "About the Shaker Sweater."

48 Josephine E. Wilson Diary, October 6–7, 1921, MS #1985.55, cited in Burks, note 19. Canterbury Shaker Village, NH.